THE COST OF

THE COST
OF COMFORT

John Lachs

Indiana University Press

This book is a publication of

Indiana University Press
Office of Scholarly Publishing
Herman B Wells Library 350
1320 East 10th Street
Bloomington, Indiana 47405 USA

iupress.indiana.edu

Manufactured in the United States of America

Cataloging information is available from the Library of Congress.

ISBN 978-0-253-04316-0 (hdbk.)
ISBN 978-0-253-04317-7 (pbk.)
ISBN 978-0-253-04318-4 (web PDF)

1 2 3 4 5   23 22 21 20 19

Contents

Preface

I HAVE LONG been fascinated by the cushioned life we lead, enjoying relative security and plenty. I have long been frustrated by the irresponsibility of people in corporations and government, creating a sense of bitterness in those they are supposed to serve. This book is an attempt to show that there is an organic connection between these two sets of experiences. Their relation is established by means of the idea of mediation, a nearly universal feature of human action.

In mediation we interpose tools or other humans between ourselves and what we want to attain. This vastly increases the scope and efficacy of our power, but at the cost of the steady increase of passivity and manipulativeness. I trace the syndrome as it shows itself in daily life, corporations, and government, and I conclude with concrete suggestions for remediation.

Intermediate Man, a book I wrote some years ago, presented similar ideas. But this book is significantly different from the earlier. It covers more topics and makes, I hope, a more compelling case for my analysis. It presents mediation in testable form, inviting experimentation to establish that its growth increases and its reduction moderates the five painful costs that attend it.

The centrality of mediation for civilized life makes it unwise if not impossible to eliminate it. Instead, we can take steps to counteract its corrosive effects and thereby significantly improve the quality of our lives. In the earlier book, I argued that suitably revised education would be adequate to overcome the worst effects of mediation. Age must have moderated my sweeping enthusiasm: here, I offer a set of more modest concrete proposals that, if instituted, would net us significant improvement.

In trying to reduce the costs of mediation, we must not overlook the pleasure some gain from the suffering of others. Those who feel impotent in dealing with large corporations delight in complaining; manipulators embrace their success; people unable to see their acts as their own enjoy not caring; irresponsible office holders acquire temporary power.

But such satisfactions are derivative and fleeting. They are nothing compared to the feeling tone of a society of caring, morally alert individuals.

If my analysis of a major source of social problems is correct, controlling many of the undesirable effects of mediation should be possible. That makes it a worthy aim not to surrender our comforts but to reduce their cost.

THE COST OF COMFORT

1 Comfort

EACH DAY, WE perform hundreds of actions. Each day, thousands of things happen to us. Some we don't notice; others we consider insignificant. By tomorrow, almost everything that took place in this ordinary today will have been forgotten; a year from now, we will probably remember nothing of it at all. Forgetting lightens the burden of existence by liberating us from the past. It leaves us with a firm sense of who we are, though little in the way of particulars.

In this way, much of what shapes our lives escapes attention or memory. Although we remember some highlights, we know little of the details of how things went for us twenty or forty years ago. We may silently suppose that, in important ways, nothing has ever been very different from what it is today. Our knowledge of history should correct such hapless suppositions, but that knowledge, too, is limited to a few dates, signal events, and a sense of general tendencies.

History would help if it were the story of how people used to live. But the daily existence of ordinary people has attracted little of the attention of historians. The stress on great persons and momentous events has made it difficult for us to relate ourselves to the people who went before. We rarely ask and cannot answer the question of what our lives would have been like had we lived fifty or five hundred years ago. We know little of how we have lived and almost nothing about the life of earlier generations. Without comparisons, we can neither understand nor assess our current condition.

Perhaps only ignorance of economics, which has ruined the Soviet Union and its affiliated republics, can match our innocence of historical reality. The present's preoccupation with itself is well symbolized by the question a college student once asked me. In speaking of self-sacrifice in the service of a cause, I used the word *kamikaze*. Was that the name, he inquired, of a new Japanese sedan? Young people appear to have trouble making the notion vivid for themselves that there were times in the history of the world when telephones and airplanes did not exist and when bananas were not available year-round. Older folks don't do much better, forgetting what they have seen with their own eyes.

This ignorance and forgetfulness disguise the marvelous accomplishments of the modern world. To be sure, the comfort and plenty created by industrial civilization have not yet reached everyone on the planet. But a growing number of humans live longer, eat better, suffer less, and satisfy more of a broader range of desires than any previous generation. The great philosopher William James recognized this trend as early as 1907, when he wrote: "We approach the wishing-cap type of organization . . . in a few departments of life. We want water and we turn a faucet. We want a kodak-picture and we press a button. We want information and we telephone. We want to travel and we buy a ticket. In these and similar cases, we hardly need to do more than the wishing—the world is rationally organized to do the rest."[1]

To this list of comforts, James could now add high-speed travel by jet plane, instant communication with virtually every part of the world, the assured supply of wholesome and varied foods, and reliable medical care, among many others. Ordinary people in industrialized countries live much better today than kings did just a few hundred years ago. Kings never enjoyed the comforts of keeping their abode at the desired temperature throughout the year and of using a multitude of products to reduce pain, enhance taste, and eliminate many of the unpleasant side effects of organic life. They shared a world of stench with bedbugs and cockroaches. Their hairy parts provided a home for lice, and their teeth slowly rotted in their jaws. Many were in poor health much of the time; when they fell seriously ill, they were treated by charlatans who bled them or offered powdered pearls as lifesaving medicine. Control over the fate of others was their compensation for the inability to control their own.

In the twelfth century, complications attending childbirth often resulted in the mother's death. Infant mortality was high; those who survived past puberty could expect to live to their thirties. Typhoid, pneumonia, and circulatory diseases of all sorts were rampant. Bad gums, ulcers, and even scurvy went largely untreated. Hordes of sick, crippled, maimed, blind, and mentally ill people roamed the grimy streets of the major cities. Disfiguring skin diseases made human bodies abhorrent to sight. Even among young people, good teeth and sweet breath were highly prized rarities.[2]

In those days, travel was undertaken by foot or on horseback. A full day's ride would carry the traveler about thirty-five miles over roads with large holes where the paving stones had been stolen. Some holes were large enough to break the leg and sometimes the neck of inattentive travelers. The journey from London to Paris required no less than seven days. It was unwise to attempt it alone: a single individual could readily fall prey to wild animals or brigands on the road.

Most houses in the twelfth century consisted of a single room, which served as kitchen, living room, and bedroom. A waste pit near the fire at one end of the room "took care of sewage as well as kitchen refuse."[3] Unlit city streets functioned as open sewers, carrying human waste to the river from which people took drinking water in pails back to their homes. As late as the seventeenth century, the Seine gave dysentery "to all except those who were natives of the region."[4]

The history of dentistry affords an insight into how far the modern world has progressed. During the Middle Ages, toothaches and diseases of the gums received no reliable treatment. Dental surgery was so dangerous that Pope Gregory II "counseled prayer and endurance of pain rather than submission to the knife."[5] As late as the sixteenth century, the extraction of a single tooth could lead to death: untrained surgeons frequently removed a portion of the jaw with the tooth, causing infection and general sepsis.[6]

To make teeth fall out so they would not have to be pulled, physicians recommended that dried cow's dung or the fluid that results from boiling small green frogs be applied to the gums.[7] Toothaches were treated by bleeding patients or by plunging hot needles into their gums and earlobes. Until the beginning of the nineteenth century, barbers and blacksmiths, who had little knowledge of anatomy or physiology, performed almost all tooth extractions.

Poor teeth and inadequate dental care made human life miserable until less than a hundred years ago. Both George Washington and his wife experienced constant dental problems. He lost all but one of his teeth and found his dentures—some of them made of ivory, others of hippopotamus tusk and gold—thoroughly unsatisfactory.[8] Good dental care, healthy diet, and the fluoridation of drinking water have so improved the teeth of young Americans that some schools of dentistry have closed and dentists are concerned about the future of their profession. This achievement constitutes an improvement in the quality of human life whose magnitude can be measured only by comparison with the pain endured by our ancestors throughout the ages.

Purists and Puritans object to the comforts we enjoy by charging that they render us soft and turn our attention from virtue and high culture to materialistic pursuits. The ills supposedly brought on by improvements in the conditions of life constitute a mighty list. They include self-indulgence, the loss of ideals, egoism, the breakdown of community values, and a vicious relativism that blinds us to the permanent differences between good and evil. Some look with admiration on groups such as the Amish that make do without modern conveniences in the name of a wholesome life. Others search for exemplars of a simple existence in the past and praise Thoreau or recommend the values of Native American tribes.

These are wayward, unfocused complaints. The modern world exacts a price for its comforts, but there is little doubt that the comforts are benefits. Nothing shows this more clearly than the fact that even those who most strongly condemn the pleasant life are reluctant to give it up. People who move to tight and clean utopian communities take their television sets with them. Evangelists inveighing against materialism fly in jet planes from city to city and stay in fine hotels. Those who want to simplify their lives rarely insist on drinking polluted water or playing host to parasites. The Amish themselves do not reject the blessings of technology—they travel in wheeled wagons, after all—they just limit these benefits to what existed at an earlier stage in the development of our skills.

Public choice is not irrelevant to determining the value of our comforts. Consistent preference of healthy food over garbage reveals something important about what is of value to human beings. The desire of people in developing countries for adequate housing, competent medical care, and private cars cannot be viewed as the expression of lamentable materialism. The unhesitating decision to stay in touch with loved ones far away suggests that such communication is not a dispensable nicety but an important part of a full human life.

In any case, it is difficult to believe that toothaches and amoebic dysentery keep one's mind on the ideal, while physical well-being leads to spiritual ruin. Does it conduce to self-indulgence not to die of childbirth at eighteen? Does it diminish our commitment to good music that everyone can hear it everywhere, rather than only the bishop and the prince in their castles? Does it reduce the quality of our conversation that we can conduct it with interesting people on the other side of the globe? The hollowness of the attack on modern life in the name of higher values is best seen by observing the behavior of spiritual masters when they get near material goods. Hindu gurus come to mind, who flock to this country to teach discipline and self-abnegation and buy Cadillac limousines with the proceeds.

The success of governments devoted to providing public sanitation and security of person and property, along with the success of economies focused on the production of consumer goods, presents powerful evidence of the importance of comfort. The level of control we have achieved over disease, accident, and the requirements of decent life enable, for the first time in the history of the world, large numbers of people to enjoy a long and satisfying existence. It is rhetorical but not exaggerated to say that any life worse than this is inappropriate for humans.

Notes

1. William James, *Pragmatism* (Indianapolis: Hackett, 1981), 130.
2. Urban Tigner Holmes, Jr., *Daily Living in the Twelfth Century* (Madison: University of Wisconsin Press, 1952), 226–27.
3. Ibid., 97.
4. Ibid., 92.
5. Malvin E. Ring, *Dentistry: An Illustrated History* (New York: H. N. Abrams, 1985), 58.
6. Ibid., 129.
7. J. A. Taylor, *History of Dentistry* (Philadelphia: Lea & Febiger, 1922), 36.
8. Ring, *Dentistry: An Illustrated History*, 193.

2 Discomfort

IN SPITE OF striking improvements in the quality of life, people in the modern world appear not to be happy. There are, as there have always been, individual reasons for unhappiness. Disappointed love and tragic accident grieve us no less than they saddened our ancestors. Arbitrary injustice has not been eliminated, and lamentable inequities remain between the sexes, between races, between the rich and the poor and the young and the old. It is true, moreover, that humans quickly forget how bad things have been, take the good for granted, and ask for more. And it may be easier to face death at thirty if we see that as natural than at eighty if we believe our power to postpone it grows daily but not fast enough.

These are legitimate sources of distress, but they explain neither the full measure of our unhappiness nor the special nature of our frustrations. For we enjoy the comforts of the world, and, although inequities rightly irritate, these pleasures offer compensation. What ails us, moreover, are not the understandable human tendencies to want more and to want not to die. Many among us know that our time must come, that we are not as well off as some of our neighbors, that terrible things can and do happen, and that our dreams cannot all come true. We can achieve a certain equanimity about these things, a peace in relation to the great and perhaps unavoidable limits of human existence. Yet we remain frustrated and unhappy about the cost of modern life. How we must live and what we must do to gain these comforts cast a dark shadow on our moods and minds.

In one sense, that we should be unhappy in the modern world is laughable. A comparison with how we would have fared in prior centuries should fill us with gratitude for having been born in the twentieth or the twenty-first century. Yet we feel a disquiet that, though ill focused, is nevertheless powerful and wrenching. Its pervasive, vague presence makes it difficult to diagnose. It gives voice to itself in grumbling about the inhumanity of the system, the impotence of the individual, and the impossibility of getting heard. We enjoy the comforts that industry provides, but we feel we have no standing in the world—to those in power, we are members of a faceless crowd. Our names are afterthoughts appended to the numbers that carry our identity and that, entered into official computers, reveal our history, financial condition, and taste. It does not take an exaggerated sense of self-importance to feel that we are drowning in the herd because, in some important yet unappreciated way, we are different from everybody else.

The discordant undertone of our experience expresses the ambivalent attitudes of the modern world to the private person. The very notion of the individual is supposed to have been invented by modern Western civilization. We celebrate the individual as essential for innovation and as the foundation of democracy. We pass laws to protect individual rights. But each private, conscious person is a unique center of activity and feeling. The focus on this experienced uniqueness slips the moment we begin to speak of *the individual*, an abstract idea that captures only what we have in common, not what makes each of us singular and special. The laws that protect individuals similarly fail to take into account the fact that, from our own perspective, every one of us constitutes an exception. Our society favors the individual only in the abstract and as a code name for the elements of the crowd; it shows little sensitivity to the specific needs and distinct feelings of particular people.

The unhappiness of the modern world, then, is of a special sort: it is closely connected to the growing insignificance of individuals. Huge institutions surround and engulf us; we feel powerless to influence their course. We finance and serve them without knowing and without being able to control what they do. We are lost in their bowels and experience much social life as a sort of homelessness. Even the institutions within which we work are difficult to embrace as our own: rules we did not make govern our roles, and what we do fails to follow from who we are. As a consequence, we feel used and manipulated and take no responsibility for the actions we perform in an official capacity. The devastating sense of the meaninglessness of what we do and of our own unimportance moves us alternately to shoulder-shrugging indifference and to personal despair.

Many of these phenomena have captured the attention of philosophers and sociologists. They invented the idea of alienation partly as a convenient summary and partly as an explanation of these experiences.

This idea, however, has never been anything but murky. In some cases, it is used to refer to a process of undesirable distancing, in others to the product of such a process. Some thinkers believe alienation is primarily subjective or psychological in nature; others attempt to find it in objective social conditions. Almost all of them remain vague about whether the notion serves as more than a shorthand for observed phenomena, about whether it has explanatory power. Since Georg Hegel's celebrated account of the unhappy consciousness, alienation theorists have been notoriously more successful at describing what occurs than at helping us understand it. The only point of general agreement is that whatever alienation may be, it is not a good thing. A value judgment is, in this way, built directly into the description of the facts, with the result that alienation comes to function as a magnet, attracting and attempting to account for all manner of unrelated ills.

The theories that have been advanced to explain the nature and causes of alienation phenomena range from the plausible to the nearly absurd. Thinkers who focus on the breakdown of community[1] are closest to the truth, although their analysis is not sufficiently penetrating. They think that the loss of traditional shared values is adequate to account for anomie. But if by "values" they mean social standards of behavior, they are wrong in supposing that there has been a loss—it is just that we must look for them in the world of work and in popular culture rather than in religion. The breakdown of community comes from the psychological side. Paradoxically, we live in ever more tightly integrated social units, yet we view these less and less as our communal homes. The breakdown is of our *sense* of community, and this is a fact to be explained rather than one that sheds light on everything else.

Marxist and Freudian theories count among the least satisfactory views. The idea that, in an age of unprecedented sexual freedom, widespread human unhappiness is due to sexual repression lacks even initial plausibility. And to suppose that our problems are due to the private ownership of the means of production is to show a stunning blindness to what those problems actually are. In any case, we have seen ample evidence that when individuals no longer own the machinery of production (as in failed Soviet state capitalism), the psychological devastation increases rather than disappears.

The record of alienation theories is not strong enough to compel us to build on it. We can make more headway if we abandon the idea altogether and start anew. This makes it possible to jettison the value commitments that go with the notion of alienation and to escape the accidental historical baggage carried by the term. It also helps us break the powerful connection the idea enjoys to a metaphysics that does not hesitate to declare what is and what is not proper for humans everywhere. Instead, we need to develop an accurate description of the nature of our unhappiness, along with a sensible, defensible, and testable account of its causes. The description and the explanation will take form concurrently. The process is similar to what happens when physicians diagnose disease: the recognition of symptoms and the formulation of hypotheses to account for them are intricately connected and proceed hand in hand.

This does not mean that our world of comfort is socially or psychologically sick. The analogy with diagnosing illness is limited, and useful mainly in two ways. The first is the manner in which, in both cases, palpable symptoms suggest hypotheses, and good hypotheses aid in uncovering additional symptoms. In both, also, the success of suggested remedies provides limited confirmation of the diagnosis.

The second value of the analogy is to remind us that our frustrations are best understood as natural events in a natural context. We know that being overweight is the normal outcome of enjoying the pleasures of food too much (or of too much food), and that hypertension and diabetes flow naturally from obesity. In just that way, the unhappiness of industrial society may well be a natural consequence of what makes for its delights. If we think along these lines, we can escape absurd conspiracy theories and the need to postulate ad hoc social malfunctions to provide an explanation. We can then see our comfort as a great benefit and our discomfort as its unavoidable cost.

Note

1. Emile Durkheim, in *Suicide* (1897), presents one version of this view. A contemporary advocate of a related line of argument is Andrew Oldenquist.

3   A Broken and an Integrated World

We live in a broken world and know not how to mend it. People downtown approach in fear; neighbors view each other with suspicion. Parents see their children as strangers in the house, and we feel isolated in human company. The sources of power are hidden from almost everyone, and we are drawn to single acts of symbolic defiance. The daily life of the world appears to consist of disconnected events without purpose or lasting issue. No one seems to understand how our efforts unite to make a greater whole and why our best hopes are abandoned or, worse, dashed. In prior years, the times may have been out of joint; today, they appear utterly dismembered.

We also live in a tightly unified world that we are anxious to escape. In our jobs and as citizens of the state, we are stapled to each other and share a common fate. Our movements are monitored, and endless regulations govern our acts. Others control what we can do, where we must yield, how we may live. Exquisitely integrated but narrow roles in gigantic institutions define and confine us; we are hemmed in on all sides. We march or stumble through a crowded world contributing to acts we never grasp, helping to cause effects no one fully knows or wants. The thought of private dignity and the hope for self-determination haunt us, but they remain unattainable.

The broken world and the tight, crowded world are organically connected. Understanding their relation is indispensable for learning what ails us and for therapy. Yet we have made remarkably little headway in the last several hundred years in giving a sensible and unified account of the concurrent growth of integration and fragmentation in society. At least one part of the reason for this is the interest in remediation. Social problems tend to be the province of social reformers, and those who wish to bring about change must identify a relatively simple and eliminable cause of our distress. If the problems of social life are the diffuse costs of living in a complex and populous world, improvement in our condition may appear elusive or impossible. The reformer, therefore, naturally seeks a single cause and a unique malfunction. In this way, ridding ourselves of one difficulty promises a resolution of all our problems.

In the real world, unfortunately, things are not this simple. Nothing solves every problem, and the utopian promise of costless benefits remains a cruel hoax. Rain makes the flowers grow but also gets us wet; it is perfectly natural, though not logically necessary, that this be so. Similarly, social problems are natural attendants of social life. This means that our comfort and discomfort hang together in an intelligible way. The philosopher's job is to formulate a theory that elucidates the connection and reduces the diversity of facts to the unity provided by just a few carefully interrelated concepts.

Let me begin with a mode of thought natural to the broken world. Analysis into atomic constituents or isolated factors yields excellent results in science. The sequence of happenings in daily life may seem continuous, yet even people who are not scientists think of it as a flow of discrete, minuscule events. For there are potential turning points everywhere: if only I had not slammed on the brakes when I hit that patch of ice, if only Othello had not believed Iago, if only Nixon had not recorded his conversations, or if the recordings had not been discovered, or if at least he had not erased them, everything, we think, would be different. In this way, we convince ourselves that our actions have crisis points, small segments or atomic units that constitute their heart.

This line of thought tends to make us lose all sense of the unity or continuity of our acts. Actions consist of intention, execution, and outcome. None of the three, not even the actual performance in isolation, is the action—the events that constitute execution acquire their character and meaning from the intention that gave birth to them and the consequences that followed. Intention insensibly flows into the early stages of the actual operation and guides its development. Consequence is ever present as well. The pleasure that scratching one's head creates is an inseparable attendant of the physical action.

Furthermore, the nature, location, and intensity of the effect determine the subsequent stage of the cause. Where the nails go next, at what speed, and how hard constitute an outcome of the initial pleasurable result. I might want to sustain the feeling, carry it to another part of the scalp, or stop satisfied. In this way, consequences guide the act no less than do intentions, and the three elements combine to form an indissoluble unity. Like the flight of the boomerang, this unified interplay of intention, actual performance, and consequences is an unbroken process. We can distinguish its parts but reap only confusion if we declare any of them more essential than the rest or identify one, such as the actual performance, with the whole.

4 Complete and Dismembered Actions

IN IDEALLY COMPLETE or at least maximally intelligible actions, the intention, performance, and attendant consequences all reside in a single agent. Noting my hunger, intending to relieve it, raiding the refrigerator, fixing a sandwich, eating it, and experiencing the pleasures of taste and then of a full stomach constitute a continuous activity. In it, I know in a preeminent, immediate way what it means to do something, what is achieved, why it is attempted, and what it takes to bring it about. This notion of the individually initiated, performed, and enjoyed (or suffered) act serves as the generating ideal of human freedom. In autonomous actions, desires lead to intentions and then to the performance of the actions we intend. John Stuart Mill and others who have not embraced metaphysical obscurities in their account of freedom have always known that it consists of the coincidence in a single person of desire and the power to act on it. In order to achieve self-determination, we need to do what we wish and welcome what we do.

Thinking of it in this way immediately reveals the natural connection between freedom and responsibility. Liberty consists of the unity or continuity of intention and performance. Responsibility, by contrast, is the undivided oneness of what we do and the consequences that flow from it. Freedom is lodged in the first phase of a complete action, in the process of converting plan into execution. Responsibility resides in the second phase and consists of the way our action changes the world, of the consequences we must bear on account of what we did. So long as the trinity of intention, performance, and outcome is centered in the agent, freedom and responsibility remain inseparable realities.

In the broken world, however, the single-agent unity of actions is shattered. Much of what I do fails to achieve the dignity of a full action, that is, of an action that I plan, that I execute, and whose consequences I bear. Throughout much of our lives, we participate as bit players in larger social acts. In such acts, these functions are assigned to different individuals or groups: a few plan or frame purposes, a large number of others execute them, and distant strangers endure or enjoy what is produced.

The provision of air service between cities might serve as an example. Many individuals contribute to making this process possible, sometimes without full knowledge of what they do, by fabricating metal and plastic parts, by calling in weather data, and by refining oil. A small number of people—presidents of corporations, schedulers, and financial analysts—serve as planners. Many more, including pilots, flight attendants, mechanics, and baggage handlers, share the burden of actually providing the service. Others, ranging from the customers who fly to those deafened near airports when the planes take off, enjoy or suffer the consequences.

Each of these main functions of planning, executing, and enjoying or suffering the results is itself divided into innumerable, minute act-fragments. Among those who provide the service, for example, some take tickets, some guide the planes to their gates, and some clean the seats when the passengers deplane. Planning and management activities are also distributed among a number of persons, some of whom make financial forecasts while others schedule the maintenance of the planes.

In this way, intending, doing, and dealing with the consequences become separate affairs occupying hundreds, in many cases thousands, of people at a physical and psychological remove from one another. None of them performs a complete human act; none has the satisfaction of acting on self-made plans and seeing the results. The social act may be tightly integrated in the service of some end and exquisitely adapted to producing desired results. But in one important respect, it is utterly dismembered. Individual participants in it, making minor and seemingly disconnected contributions, experience it as fragmented and deprived of meaning. They perform narrow tasks, know little of what fellow workers are doing, and cannot understand how such isolated act-fragments make a useful whole.

The collaborative social act can accomplish much more than any single act or collection of isolated actions performed by an individual. This power makes the social act the foundation of our comfort. Without the rationally structured cooperative efforts of people, we could not purify water, generate electricity, or manufacture steel. Without the intelligent integration of large-scale social acts, grocery stores would run out of food, and hospitals could get no medicines.

The continued existence of communities as we know them depends on the reliable availability of the goods and services produced by an entire system of social acts. If even a part of the system, say that devoted to the distribution of manufactured products, were impaired, chaos would follow. If the system as a whole were to fail altogether in even one place, wholesale disaster would be difficult to avoid. Imagine the inhabitants of New York City fanning out over the countryside in an attempt to provide individually for their basic needs!

Breaking the social act into its minute constituent parts and assigning each of them to a different individual creates pervasive ignorance. Those who contribute to the performance of the acts find both the plan they execute and the ultimate results hidden from their ken. This means that, strictly speaking, they know neither what they do nor why. People on whom the consequences fall live in frustration. Since they have no access to the design and performance of the acts that shape their lives, they see only unexplained windfalls and abrupt catastrophes. The planners are in the best position to understand the entire process, but they normally lack direct experience of how their ideas fare in reality. Their social distance, measured by the number of facilitating agents between them and the embodiment of what they intend, denies them direct experience of the nature, circumstances, costs, and outcome of what is done. Without such firsthand experience, they cannot grasp how and why their plans are distorted in the execution and how they affect people far away.

The lack of direct experience is of central importance here. Planners and leaders tend to have little idea of the way their designs are carried out. Legislators, administrators, and bureaucrats make rules whose application rests in other hands and whose effects are unpredictable. Decision makers and those who put their ideas into practice enjoy too little personal contact to understand each other's problems, circumstances, and points of view. Executives tend to be so shielded from knowledge of their plans' effects on individual persons that they can experience little sympathy for those who suffer in the process.

Results are considered only in the aggregate and on statistical individuals; the effects of actions on the feeling subject, on the private soul, remain unobserved and hence not parts of the calculation. As a result, those on the receiving end (and in one context or another, that includes all of us) find the entire process of making decisions and executing them unintelligible or unintelligent. Since it is easiest to explain untoward happenings as due to malice, we begin to fancy that the world is bent on frustrating our will. Institutions and those who occupy positions in them thus come to be viewed with suspicion, and social life acquires an undertone of resentment and fear.

The fragmentation of the social act occurs in proportion to its size and complexity. Generally, the more momentous and remarkable human purposes become, the more people are needed to accomplish them. These individuals operate in a highly organized way, each making a contribution to the larger act that none could perform alone. Paradoxically yet naturally, an increase in the integration of the social act brings with it a corresponding growth in psychic fragmentation. Simply put, social integration leads to psychological fragmentation.

From the social perspective, for now at least and for the most part, everything appears to be working effectively and well. But the disconnectedness is evident when we view the situation from the standpoint of the individual. The two perspectives are inseparably connected. The increase in the size of our institutions is precisely what reduces the scope and significance of individual contribution. The complexity of social life is what submerges us in a sea of incomprehension.

The broken world is, in this way, the psychological counterpart of the tightly ordered world of large-scale social acts. This, on first analysis, is the private cost of public good: the great wealth and stability of industrial society are created at the expense of the passivity and psychic impoverishment of its members. This pauperization is not to be measured by the standards of high culture, by the absence from our souls of refined taste and clever speculations. We lack basic orientation about the world and our place in it. The loss of self-respect and self-understanding—the loss of self—this entails steals meaning and dignity from daily life.

5 Mediation

Participants in the integrated social act experience their own activity as fragmented and meaningless. Since they perform incomplete human acts, they gain little individual satisfaction from them. From an objective standpoint, of course, they make indispensable contributions to the production of goods and services. Institutions and the social acts of which they consist are integrated sets of cooperative activities. In them, large numbers of individuals pool their skills and efforts in the service of a goal none could achieve alone. The pervasive reality in industrial, commercial, political, and even professional life, therefore, is collaboration in the form of making a small, relatively specialized contribution to a larger whole.

The fact that the contribution of each person is minuscule and presupposes the work of many others places us in a special relation to our fellows. We cannot perform complete human actions without them. We must have them surround us on all sides, filling the gaps between desired outcomes and the little we can do. To the extent that the social acts in which I participate are mine, other people help me perform my actions. Since the acts also belong to them, however, I in turn aid them with theirs. Each of us relies on the others for planning or execution or savoring the results. None of us can accomplish anything of social significance without the continued participation of all the rest.

In large-scale actions, then, others are interposed between me and the outcome of my acts. I find myself in a similar position, occupying a place between others and the results of their endeavors. I shall call this interposition of others between oneself and the complete act (which includes the consequences) *mediation*. A simple form of such interposition is doing something for another specifically upon request. But mediation does not require deliberate personal interaction. In its institutionalized forms, particularly in mass society, complex and indispensable social acts are performed on behalf of many without anyone having asked for them. No one munching on a sandwich has ever asked an Iowa farmer to invest in steers, yet from farm to kitchen, many thousands work to keep fries coming and hamburger buns filled.

Social institutions consist of chains of mediation—human beings connected to one another by performing actions on each others' behalf. We function in the chains as if we had a tacit contract with each other. Each person makes a small contribution to what is of benefit to some or all, in return for what is needed for a comfortable life. In a sense, though for the most part without consciousness of it, we use others as tools to make our existence secure and pleasant, and we offer them in payment the opportunity of using us. Primitive humans interposed sticks and rocks between themselves and what was to be done; we thrust an entire system of intermediary agents and machines between ourselves and our actions. The difference is only in quantity of mediation, which affects the quality of life.

Mediation in its social form is simple human cooperativeness. We constantly find ourselves doing things for others and, in turn, relying on others to meet our needs and satisfy our wants. We mediate the actions of others when we act in their stead or on their behalf; we do this frequently to enhance their power, relieve their burdens, or increase their convenience. Parents mediate the actions of their infants; barbers, of their customers; gas company employees, of everyone who wishes to keep warm.

In small social groups, cooperation can take the form of doing the job together. In populous societies, it is impractical or impossible for us to be present at every place where others act on our behalf. Cooperation then becomes shared participation in diverse phases of some larger social act—an ill-understood, momentous exchange of services. In this situation, we do not know the precise nature and do not have immediate experience of what others do for us. As social institutions grow, we lose sight even of the fact that others labor on our behalf. The physical and institutional distance at which they operate from us makes them disappear from our ken; we are left in ignorance of the conditions of our life and weal.

Mediation takes many forms. For example, what I interpose between myself and the end I wish to gain need not be another human being. In its primitive form, mediation is simply the use of a tool to shield the body or to enhance effectiveness. The gloves I wear when I prune the rosebush are interposed between thorns and living flesh; they are the means used to protect my hands. Carpenters find it advantageous to drill the holes needed for bolts instead of trying to make them by scraping the wood with their nails. What makes these cases of mediation is the placement of a third between oneself and the object one works on or the result one attempts to achieve. The employment of instruments and means—the interposition of such mediating thirds—has served as the foundation of civilized life from its beginnings. Spears and stones occupied a central position between early humans and the animals they hunted, just as the knife still does between the cook and his pot roast.

When the third I interpose between intention and accomplishment is an inert tool in need of manipulation by me, the cognitive distance between agent and consequence remains minimal. After all, I prune the rosebush, and I drill the hole; my tools have no independent life. They work when I put them to work, and I know firsthand everything that is done and how it gets accomplished. To be sure, a little cognitive slippage does seep in: dentists learn the full nature of what they do only when the drill slips from the tooth and strikes their hand. But such ignorance of some dimensions of what we do is fairly easily corrected; so long as intention, act, and consequence all reside in a single agent, experience can provide the remedy.

Things change when inert tools span distances or become so complex that they acquire a life of their own. Pilots, flying high above the clouds, adjust gauges and push buttons to drop their bombs. To be sure, the instruments operate without the bombardiers as little as a hammer on its own pounds nails. But the immense sophistication of the tools and the distance they introduce between agent and ultimate effect deny bombardiers the experience of what they bring about. Even if they understand how the machines work, they lack vivid, immediate acquaintance with what they cause—they cannot even imagine the carnage on the ground. Such ignorance is sometimes disguised by job descriptions and general verbal accounts. But language itself is a mediating tool that works least well when used as a substitute for experience.

The cognitive or psychic distance between agent and consequence is greatest when the instruments we use to fulfill our desires are other human beings. Even a single person acting on our behalf can make it difficult for us to know what is accomplished and at the cost of what undesirable side effects. The independent agency of others naturally takes them beyond our intentions and out of our sight. The reports we receive of deeds performed on our behalf at a distance lack the richness and immediacy of witness. But here at least we are honored with reports. By contrast, when mediation becomes large scale and institutionalized, no one discloses what is done for us or how. Of course, in many cases nothing is performed for any one of us uniquely. When I contract for electrical service, for example, people do not rush out to make me some power. The thousands of people employed by the company simply generate electricity, and some of it can be for me if I agree to pay. So although they do not do it specifically for me, yet they do it for me and others and never tell us how or at what cost. As a result, I can sit in a well-lit, air-conditioned home, unmindful of strip mining and global warming.

We can mediate the actions of others whether or not we intend to do so or are even aware of doing it. Turning off the lights of a friend's parked car is a case of mediation; if I did not do it, it would fall to the owner to return. But contributing to the manufacture of one of the roughly eighteen thousand parts needed to make a car is mediation also, even though the act is performed on behalf of unknown future buyers. In large-scale society, structures and institutions replace private intentions. Therefore, those who work for a corporation need not mean to help and do not have to know its clients or its products in order to find themselves usefully interposed between management and profitable sales.

Much of industrial and commercial life consists of the introduction of mediating agencies. Distributors and sales organizations act as connecting third parties between producers and consumers. Bankers serve as the linkage between savers and borrowers. Real estate agents build bridges between sellers and buyers. We can think of such thirds as tools in the hands of the people they connect. Given the power of mediating agencies, however, this view is often misleading. It is altogether inaccurate when the mediators are vast institutions that conjoin sets of individuals. A grocery chain that buys from farmers in a number of countries and sells to customers in a hundred cities is not an instrument that can be made to do the will of either group. And even though institutions consist of chains of mediation, single or small groups of workers in them hold little power to make them change their ways.

One way to think about the history of humankind is as the story of the growth of mediation. The fundamental difference between primitive tools to make life better and the vast system of institutions in which we live and move and have our being is the size and complexity of mediating agencies. In the years since our ancestors first started using stone implements and fire, the principle or process of interposing powers between the self and the world has not changed. The momentous improvements in life are due to how we have learned to protect ourselves and to pursue our desires. Only the nature of what we place between ourselves and our goals—that is, the sophistication of our mediating thirds—has changed. We have moved from relying on primitive physical implements to using the coordinated efforts of vast collections of human beings. Instead of carrying stout sticks and stone hatchets, we now entrust our safety to the police. Instead of running after wild animals with spears, we buy food produced, processed, packaged, and put on the shelf by countless others.

Large numbers of humans now make advanced instruments, such as oil refineries, and many others apply them to our benefit and on our behalf. The interconnected system of mediating tools that ensures the modern world's comfort thus includes both skilled human activities and material objects subtly adapted to serve our ends. The savage beat a path through the wilderness; we drive along highways built by faceless multitudes, in cars to whose production tens of thousands of people contributed, using oil and gas others discovered, pumped, refined, and transported to town. There is a momentous difference here, and yet there is none. None, because both the savages and we enjoy the benefits of mediation. Momentous, because they had only their arms and knives and legs to make the path, while we employ the efforts of an organized world to smooth our way.

6 Philosophical Excursion

Hegel and Peirce on Mediation

THE PLACEMENT OF a third between self and other, the employment of instruments, the introduction of means to achieve ends—mediation, in short—constitutes an indispensable condition of human life. The centrality of such activity was not fully appreciated until the nineteenth-century German philosopher Hegel's wholesale celebration of its virtues. Hegel saw mediation as all-pervasive—he thought that only negativity and the developmental stages to which it gives rise make the growth of consciousness, of organized human life, possible. The American thinker Charles Sanders Peirce, under Hegel's influence, declared mediation or thirdness the category of rationality and announced that its increase is the ultimate evolutionary aim of the universe.

Hegel's vision of the ubiquity of mediation is not without basis. Co-operative labor involves the introduction of empowering others between one's project and achievement. Our institutions are sets of collaborative acts frozen into mediating structures. The language of communication consists of thirds—sounds and written marks or words and sentences—bridging the gap between minds. Inference, the work of thought, is itself a mediating process that attains conclusions by means of rules or inter-jacent premises.

In his *Phenomenology of Spirit*, Hegel showed how sensation, our primitive immediacy with the world, is overcome early in the growth of thought. He maintained that as mediation or universal rational process evolves, all immediacy is transcended. This may explain why the last section of the *Phenomenology*, which presents the tantalizing promise of absolute knowledge, is so devastatingly disappointing. For such absolute understanding turns out to be no more than the sum of prior developments with no additional insight that may be savored by the private mind. On Hegel's view, sophisticated intellects should not need such an immediate feel of things. He allowed that the monarch represents the objective unity of the state in a form that is directly accessible to those mired in subjectivity. But he was clear that this palpable symbol is inadequate to the reality for which it stands and is, in any case, of significance only to ordinary people incapable of higher thought.

This rejection of immediacy entangled Hegel in a thicket of mistakes. He failed to do justice to consciousness as actually lived, to that flow of unreflective and unverbalized awareness of which much of everyday life consists. As a result, he left no room in his system for the privacy and individuality that escape description in universal terms, but that constitute the heartbeat of personal consciousness. And because of this misunderstanding of the nature of consciousness, he thought he could assign it to institutions, to states, and to an abstract, cosmic spirit seeking self-realization in history. Misplacing consciousness led him to misplace the source of agency as well—he thought that concepts, social forces, and such impersonal abstractions as reason are the ultimate sources of whatever takes place.

An adequate theory of mediation must rectify these errors. It must strike a proper balance between mediation and immediacy, assuming at the proper times the perspective of individual awareness. It must limit the assignment of consciousness to living animals alone. And it must lodge agency where it rightfully belongs, on the ontological level of particular persons. Without this, social life cannot be seen to have private costs at all. The truth is that "the litany of lamentations" of which, from the standpoint of suffering individuals, so much of history consists, constituted for Hegel neither loss nor cost. For he viewed the pain in its objectivity, the way scientists observe the death-struggle of flies caught in a spider's web or well-fed generals the discomfort of their starving soldiers. But suffering merely seen and described loses its hurt; it ceases to be pain. Without proper attention to the private soul, without deep sympathy for how things feel, theories of alienation remain laughable.

Peirce called himself a Hegelian. There are a number of reasons why the designation is appropriate. Fortunately, however, Peirce's faith in the power of thought did not blind him to the reality and importance of immediacy. He knew that Hegel went too far in denying all immediacy and, with it, the significance or even the possibility of a private, subjective life. Fortunately, Peirce corrected Hegel's tragic denial. He saw that the qualitative feel of things is an ineliminable and unsublatable element of life. His categorial scheme testifies to his belief in the irreducibility of direct experience.

He called such immediate feelings and private apprehensions "firsts" and spoke of them, at least in some places, as necessary conditions of thoughts, laws, or "thirds." With the faithfulness to experience for which he is rightly celebrated, he went so far as to note that even the most exalted thoughts have a certain inexpressible feel to consciousness—in other words, even thirds have firsts. One is tempted to speculate what the last section of the *Phenomenology of Spirit* would be like had Peirce written it. But, of course, Peirce knew that it could not be written: absolute knowledge would not emerge, he thought, until the completion of infinitely extended inquiry. Was part of his reason for lodging the fulfillment of thought in the indefinite future his realization that no finite mind could accommodate the feel of such omniscience?

Peirce's work in semiotics shows the same respect for irreducible immediacy as we find in his metaphysical speculations. When he discussed signification, he spoke not only of energetic and logical interpretants (seconds and thirds) but also of the emotional interpretant, which is the feeling produced by a sign. Moreover, when he came to distinguish the properties of signs, he was not satisfied to note their "pure demonstrative application" (their physical connection with their object) and their properly cognitive representative function. He also identified their "material qualities," which are the characters they possess in themselves or the way they appear when they stand naked in human consciousness. Direct experiences of this sort, such as the all-pervasive aroma of oranges on Christmas morning, defy analysis, explanation, or even adequate description in words. Yet their reality is undeniable, and Peirce accordingly announced that "the Immediate . . . the Unanalyzable, the Inexplicable, the Unintellectual runs in a continuous stream through our lives."[1]

In spite of Peirce's commendable focus on the way things feel to us, immediacy continues to receive little attention in the world of thought. In philosophy, in semiotics, in law and the other professions, thirds occupy pride of place. Our interest is focused on rules and laws, on the intelligible structure of what we do. We seem to think that understanding is possible on the basis of description alone and that living, direct experience, what we might call direct acquaintance, is an impediment to thought. In our urgency to know the outcome of our acts, we overlook how they feel. We appear not to realize that some of the most important consequences we help cause are feelings and emotions. Instead, we relegate private experience to the realm of the "merely subjective" and thereby rob it of dignity and significance. Even worse, some philosophers go so far as to deny the existence of feelings and private minds altogether. In the quiet of their minds, they clearly feel good about holding such positions.

Our disregard of firsts is so thorough that we are unaware of the magnitude of the loss this involves. John Dewey, who accepted Peirce's account of firsts, called such immediate experiences and ideas that which is "had." He thought that in the form of direct enjoyments, these moments constitute the only delights or consummations of which we are capable. They are, in this way, the core of value and goodness: all the instrumentalities of life aim at securing and extending these periods of gratification. Dewey's point is as right as it seems forgotten. Pleasure, satisfaction, enjoyment, and delight can exist only in being had: they are moments of life that can be shared but not expressed, experienced but not explained. In overlooking immediacy, therefore, we decline to pay attention to the values that make our existence worthwhile. If everything is merely a means to some distant objective, we are left with no intrinsically enjoyable ends at all. If everything is public activity and busy work, we are robbed of exhilaration, of joyful absorption in the moment, of the private smile of the soul.

Note

1. Charles S. Peirce, *Collected Papers*, 8 vols. (Cambridge, MA: Harvard University Press, 1931–58), 5:287.

7   Six Consequences of Mediation

We shall see that many problems of large-scale industrial society line up along this axis of immediacy and mediation. On the one hand, mediated chains enable us to accomplish staggering feats: we extract oil from the depths of the sea and send humans into space. As the chains become ever larger and more closely integrated, we manage to achieve hitherto unthinkable control over nature. Human health has improved, life expectancy has grown, and comfort has increased in the last hundred years far more than the boldest visionary would have dared to predict. These are achievable wherever people organize themselves to act in mediated chains on each others' behalf. The gains are directly correlated to the size and complexity of the chains: greater social unities can perform more stunning social feats. Mediation provides benefits so vast that without it, life would yield us mainly misery. It is the sole foundation and guaranty of our comfort.

On the other hand, the good life exacts a price. The dark side of our productive, integrated chains is the broken world of shriveled selves. For every benefit of mediation, we shoulder a matching cost. The social benefits and their private costs come in a single package: they are all natural— that is, unintended and not extraordinary—consequences of mediation. An increase in one brings with it a corresponding expansion of the other.

Mediation extends the power of individuals and the reach of their influence. The more my power is enhanced by chains of intermediaries, however, the less control I have over what is done on my behalf and— being but a small link in the chain—the less I can direct my own life. In this way, more power inevitably leads to less.

The modern world surrounds us with opportunities. At work and in the home, it offers, even demands, endless rounds of busy activity. By an odd inversion, however, the more we do, the less satisfaction we find. Because intention, execution, and enjoyment of the results of our acts do not reside in any one of us, the more active we get, the more passive we come to feel.

In mediated chains, our coworkers are partners in a shared enterprise. We collaborate and rely on one another to attain mutually desirable ends. This appreciation, however, also shows a double face: though we cooperate, we touch only to get things done. Interest in other members of a mediated chain is primarily interest in their utility, in their function as means to what we want. Humane collaboration has dehumanizing manipulativeness as its dark side and unavoidable product.

Through computers and satellites and fax machines, mediation opens the distant world. Instant access to all manner of information promises knowledge without limits. The exploits of strangers on the other side of the globe so fill our minds, however, that we fail to examine the meaning of our own acts. Disconnected facts and secondhand reports close our eyes to direct experience, and we lose appreciation for the richness of the immediate. Growing knowledge thus begets ignorance.

Mediated chains in government and business, operating by precise and impartial rules that can withstand public scrutiny, provide predictable and fair treatment for all. For the first time in history, institutions today begin to embody the respect each person deserves and the responsibility to treat everyone in a humane way. Functionaries in the chain, however, find it difficult to appropriate its actions. Because they perform incomplete acts, they learn to follow the letter of the rules and take no responsibility for anything beyond what a narrow conception of their roles demands. Humane principles thus come to be applied in an inhumanly rigid way. Responsibility defined by job description leads, in this way, to irresponsibility if we measure actions in personal terms or by their decency.

How can powerlessness, passivity, manipulation, ignorance, psychic distance, and irresponsibility all be natural accompaniments of something as beneficial as mediation? Though this may seem initially puzzling, it is not difficult to understand. A single person performing actions on my behalf beyond my sight and hearing is adequate to keep me in the dark about what is done and how, and whether I would do no differently myself. An entire chain of intermediaries, consisting perhaps of a hundred thousand people involved in mining coal and generating electricity, is too vast to be experienced and too complex to be readily understood. The actions necessary for the desired result are so numerous and so distant from me that I know little or nothing of them. They are distant not only in that they are physically remote or institutionally removed, but also because, as a result of this, they fall outside the range of my direct experience, making it difficult for me to form a meaningful idea of them.

We can see, then, that large-scale mediation significantly increases the integration of society, while it constricts, or at least fails proportionately to increase, the individual's experience and understanding. Cooperative action builds ever greater social unities. Minds, by contrast, cannot be compounded. The growth of institutions is not matched, therefore, by the development of some larger, public consciousness. Private, personal awareness is the only sort there is, and its categories remain those of individual agent and complete human act.

So, while the social world expands, the world of private reflection and understanding contracts relative to it. This discrepancy between psychological and social reality means that the ordinary person comprehends less and less of the interconnections of institutional life. And the less we know, the more we feel frustrated and shunted to the side. Innocent ignorance is the ground of much emotional disorder, and it is seeing just such disarray that leads us to believe that the cost of public good is private pain.

It might indeed appear that the benefits of mediation are social, while its costs are borne by private individuals. That is the way many of us perceive the course of the modern world. Improvements in such public goods as sanitation and control over infectious disease tend to be accompanied by an increase in alienation, unhappiness, and the incidence of mental illness. Greater social wealth seems correlated with ever more impoverished personalities. The integration of the social world appears to fragment our psychological unity, and we feel as if we were strangers, even though we work together every day.

This perception contains a grain of truth. But the sharp contrast between public and private will not stand scrutiny. In the final analysis, it is simplistic to say that in the mediated world, public benefits are bought with private grief. First, in a strict sense, there are no *public* benefits. Second, the disorder we face is far from solely private.

Since there is no such single being as the public, there can be no public benefits. To speak of them is to invoke an agreeable fiction or to use shorthand to refer to the good of a collection of individuals. By saying that a collection is a community, we do not add another entity to the individuals constituting it, but simply indicate their relation to one another. The public consists of individuals, and only the individuals are real. They alone enjoy a conscious direction to life; therefore, they alone can be benefited or harmed. The point is obvious if we look at it with clear, non-Hegelian eyes. When an infectious disease is eliminated, it is not some faceless Leviathan, the public, that is free of it, but simply you and I. In this way, public benefits are the benefits of many private persons; the good that comes of mediation is no less yours and mine than are its noxious side effects.

The disorder in the world, moreover, is not merely psychological. The inner and the outer, feeling and behavior, are not separate chambers without a door. Personal disorder shows itself in what we do, and what happens to our bodies shapes the mind. Passivity is a condition of our souls *and* of our public behavior. Psychic distance is a mode in which we experience the world, but it quickly leads to irresponsible action. The fragmented world may have started in our hurting, private psyches, but it did not remain there for long. It has invaded the integrated world and now lives in its heart. Our great institutions are staffed by too few who care, and many employees lack initiative. We are cynical of ideals that could move us, and we treat each other with suspicion or ill will. Public and private are like an old couple: in spite of disagreements, they are never far apart.

For this reason, if we could reduce the costs of mediation, we would do more than relieve subjective discomfort. To bring private consciousness more closely in line with the structure of social reality, we must acquaint people with divergent parts of the mediated chain in which they serve and help them understand how their act-fragments contribute to this greater whole. Since the subjective and the objective are inextricably interwoven, better grasp of one's social function is likely to lead to more responsible and more humane discharge of it.

As mediation increases, so do its costs. In addition to the increments in manipulation, passivity, sense of impotence, ignorance, psychic distance, and irresponsibility attributable directly to growth in the size and pervasiveness of mediated chains, these costs also enhance each other. Being manipulated, for example, fosters passivity, and psychic distance reinforces our feeling of impotence. All of them, in turn, render irresponsibility an attractive response, which again aids passivity and makes manipulation appear alright.

The total syndrome imposes a cost on modern life that is by no means negligible. Stern moralists, who delight in thinking that we tend to deceive ourselves, represent our comfort as decadent or evil and our discomfort as healthy because bracing. Such views are rightly unconvincing to the rest of us. The shared judgments of ordinary people reveal the good more reliably than do the opinions of self-appointed experts. Those of us who have had to please petty bureaucrats, who were treated as though they had no feelings or at least none that mattered, who lived the rage of impotence against the might of institutions know what comfort costs. The great social world pampers us with its goods the way rain soaks freshly planted wheat in the fields. Like the rain, it takes no interest in exceptions and offers nothing to individual need.

8 (A) Passivity

In the mediated world of large institutions, people are busier than ever. Our hunting ancestors had to expend a great deal of time on procuring food and securing their caves or huts. But they were not *busy*; single tasks occupied their time, and they were not pulled in multiple directions by conflicting obligations. Busy-ness is a creation of the modern world that presents us with untold opportunities and duties. As our power and the sphere of our operations expand, so do our choices and the demands placed on us. Job responsibilities take up the bulk of the day; family and friends vie for time in the evenings and on weekends; volunteer activities require attention; the promise of meetings has to be honored; distant relationships must be fostered; television beckons; emails and text messages wait for responses; the car must be fixed and the checkbook balanced; bills have to be paid and the dogs taken for their shots.

Some manage to glory in such a life of miscellaneous duties. Many more feel overwhelmed and look for rescue in a week of vacation. But breaks also are full of demands and obligations, and the round of things to do appears never to let up. One might think that it is a delight to have so many choices and such varied activities, but that is not how a life of busy-ness is perceived. Even though what we do is in some sense voluntary, it is not embraced as a matter of choice. What we choose we seek and affirm with a positive attitude or desire. Doing what the boss demands, painting the living room yet another color, and entertaining uninvited relatives are not chosen in that sense: we do them because something makes them necessary or important, and avoiding them would be too costly.

We do what is expected of us, but the source of our activities does not reside in us. Though we do things, we feel that we sing someone else's tune: countless others claim possession of our souls. As a result, we feel passive in our activities and active only when we are left alone to do what we really want. The feeling of passivity is easy to explain. So long as others set the parameters of our lives and determine our daily activities, it is difficult not to feel put upon. The bosses of one's own institution; functionaries of organizations, such as the electric company, with which one has to deal; and officials at every level of government exact a tribute of daily compliance with their rules.

The feeling of passivity in jobs is reinforced by passivity in entertainment. Television counts as a classically passive medium: it requires little of us beyond sitting with open eyes. Attending sport events is no better. Although football can release powerful aggressions, its efficacy usually stops at cussing and jumping up and down. Only rarely are there fisticuffs in the stands, and the police quickly stop disturbances. Active expressions of what we want and self-originated emotions are no longer necessary in a well-organized and well-controlled society. Through extensive mediation, everything is put in place for a compliant world.

We are by nature active and self-moving beings. Difficult as it is to be self-reliant, we enjoy making plans and acting on them or doing things the way we want. Such relatively unfettered freedom is hard to come by but deeply needed, and therefore the satisfaction attending it is keenly missed. Without freedom, existence feels frustrating, though we may not know exactly why. The frustration tends to spread and infect all areas of life, making people vaguely dissatisfied with their condition. The advice to do something one truly desires works only temporarily because it is set against the daily grind of work and annoying contacts with mediated institutions.

Professionals working solo appear to be the shining exception to the frustrations of passivity. Physicians and lawyers in business for themselves can set the times and terms of their practice. They have no bosses and consequently do not have to do what they don't want. Their self-determination is as broad as our society allows because, at least concerning their professional lives, they can make some decisions, act on them, and enjoy the results. Yet even these individuals are not free of passivity. Doctors have to have admitting privileges to hospitals, where they run into all the painful effects of mediated systems. If they take Medicare patients, they have to navigate the Byzantine payment method of the government. Lawyers must deal with the courts and endure the maddening inefficiencies of that bureaucracy. Both in their professional and in their private lives, therefore, they end up sharing the helplessness of the rest of us. In our world, the consequences of mediation cannot be escaped.

9 (B) Impotence

THE SENSE OF passivity can readily turn into a feeling of bitter impotence. Mediation separates intention from execution and its consequences and assigns each to different groups of individuals. Chains of mediation involve large numbers of people and encompass the distinctions between manufacturing and selling, research and investment, and travel and finance. Multinational corporations leap over national boundaries and eliminate the difference between local and global practices. The more extensive the chains, however, the more unwieldy they become. Managers on the scene lack the authority to make necessary changes; those who could adjust procedures tend to be far away and overwhelmed with other responsibilities. The result is universal frustration. Functionaries in the chain learn not to care, and aggrieved customers, clients, and—since governments are also mediated chains—citizens live with quiet resentment.

Here is a true story to illustrate the impotence customers experience. I once bought a blanket in a large department store on sale. When I opened the package at home, I found a hole right in its middle. Upon taking the blanket back, I was informed that I had purchased an item on final sale. There was no indication of this at the time, and the sales receipt did not reflect it. In an attempt at humor, I reminded the clerk that I had wanted only one thing—a blanket—but got two—a blanket and a hole; I was there to return the hole. The clerk did not find this funny. I asked for the manager; she was out to lunch. I asked for the name and address of the company's president; the clerk knew only that he was far away, but did not know exactly where. Ever more annoyed, the clerk blurted out: "Why do you pick on me? I only work here." "How thoughtless of me," I responded, "I should have complained to someone who doesn't."

I continue to feel the impotence that surrounds this experience. There was simply no way for me to get hold of the institution and make it respond to my need. The indifference of the clerk, the absence of a responsible party, and the unreachable distance of the president combined to create an impenetrable shield for the company. The only action I could take was to promise never to buy anything from that company again, but judging by how it flourishes, the resolve was itself just an expression of my angry impotence. Individuals who deal with such giant mediated chains find that often they receive scant attention. Those who complain are easily dismissed as cranks or troublemakers. Companies consider their good as a separate affair from what they offer their customers, and they are supremely confident that their brand will survive the unhappy protests of a few malcontents.

In theory, companies have to be responsive to the needs and desires of their customers. In reality, this happens relatively rarely. The reason is not ill will or a desire to frustrate the people whose business they solicit. Instead, they find it difficult or impossible to bring all the far-flung branches and distant employees of the chain into compliance. Further, special treatment of individuals is expensive and does not yield efficient results. Corporations, therefore, do not want to empower their customers; the focus is on crowds, at the expense of single persons. The grand rhetoric of the customer being king is no more than talk. It is one thing to accommodate people in general and something altogether different to attend to the needs of individual persons.

The impotence repeats itself with a vengeance in our relationships to government. With commercial corporations, individuals can opt out. They can take their business to the competition or altogether refuse to purchase goods of a certain kind. In the case of government, refusing support is impossible. There is no competing organization, and taxes are compulsory for everyone who earns a living wage. Moreover, government has a monopoly on power: it can strip people of their liberty, property, and even life, if necessary with the support of guns. No individual or group can do this without bringing down on itself the combined force of the police, the National Guard, and the Army. Although our system operates on the basis of a separation of powers, from the standpoint of the individual, the legislative, executive, and judicial functions are equally distant and equally difficult to motivate.

Government consists of interlocking systems of mediation. Since it deals with hundreds of millions of people, its laws, rules, and regulations are rigid and rarely if ever allow for exceptions. Viewed from this perspective, one can gain a better understanding of bribery. It is recognition of the inefficiency and impersonality of government processes and a desperate cry to get something personally vital done. Of course, a system of bribes puts poor people at a competitive disadvantage to those with resources, and it leads to both injustices and inefficiencies. But the point is not to recommend such a system but to understand it, and the unapproachable distance and mechanical rule-following of government officials go a long way toward explaining why those who grew up in a world of bribery find it effective and humane.

I once served, for a short time, on a university committee that considered appeals. Its work was strikingly easy: the appeals were all turned down because they asked for immunity in violating the rules. The point that the function of appeals committees is precisely to decide when a variance is appropriate fell on deaf ears. Those who think the rules are sacrosanct will never want to acknowledge that exceptions are necessary for the system to be generous and the world humane. The problem with rigid systems is that those living under them do not get a hearing. They may feel that they have a legitimate grievance, but they see no way in which their cause can prevail. They may not even know where in the wilderness of government agencies they should appeal. This is where "the constituent service" of senators and representatives comes in. That service, when it works, raises citizens out of anonymity to a position where they have to be dealt with as living, feeling persons with special needs. The trouble with this service is that few know about it, and few can be accommodated under its aegis. It would be splendid if our representatives spent more of their time mediating our relations to the government.

This of course is not how things stand today. Individuals with grievances tend to be bounced from bureau to agency and often left without satisfactory solution to their problems. Many give up on trying to prevail and would gladly settle for a sympathetic hearing followed by an explanation of why things cannot be the way they want. When even this is denied them, their frustration leads to disillusion or to violence. In their impotence, many begin to think that Congress consists of ineffective, selfish politicians and that government is an oppressive force. The alternative is even more ominous. We saw it in California a few years ago, when a man who felt he had never had a fair hearing burst into the office of a local politician and shot him dead. In the mediated world, social impotence breeds personal violence.

10 (C) Ignorance

MEDIATED CHAINS MAKE specialization in research possible, leading to an explosion of knowledge. This, in turn, creates and is enhanced by the development of sophisticated tools of communication, enabling us to pool results and to be in touch with people at the far corners of the earth. In the Middle Ages, information about health, economic developments, and political life were largely unavailable. Means of communication were lacking, and knowledge, representing power, was carefully guarded. For the most part, people did not grasp the liberating power of knowledge and hence satisfied themselves with information concerning narrowly local conditions.

The invention of printing made knowledge more widely distributed, but it still remained the precious possession of the privileged few who were able to read. Universal (and compulsory) education nearly eliminated illiteracy and to a degree leveled the field in the search for knowledge. The invention of the telegraph, the telephone, the television, the fax machine, and a rich variety of powerful digital devices made information nearly free. We are flooded with more bits of it than we can conceivably use and can access billions of facts with a few clicks on a handheld device. Search engines lead us to the wisdom of the ages, and before long information about every living human being will be enshrined and readily available in our computers. We live in a knowledge-based society whose nature and dangers we do not yet fully understand. But we know more than any previous generation, and in bold moments we suppose that before long we will know everything worth considering.

The breadth of our knowledge and the level of control we exercise over the world generate heady hopes. Our success leads to dangerous extrapolations. For example, reputable scientists believe that since we have conquered some diseases, we will be able to defeat them all. Because we have raised average life expectancy from 40 years to roughly 80, we hear predictions that this trend will continue, and we will be intact and vigorous when we are 150 years old. Past experience should have convinced us that extrapolations hardly ever work, but the sense that knowledge solves all problems and is easily obtained makes us innocent optimists.

One problem growing out of our love affair with knowledge is the conviction that everything is worth knowing. This is best expressed in social media and in blogging, with their detailed triviality. Schooling used to teach perspective. Students were expected to learn what was of significance and what did not need to be remembered. Education placed us in the midst of intellectual giants and did not permit the illusion that our ideas were of much significance.

Those days appear to be gone. With the aid of ready access to the Internet, anyone can memorialize any set of experiences. This is one of the consequences of the new power to publish one's own writing, no matter how undistinguished, and thereby call attention to one's ideas, no matter how shopworn. Not so many years ago, publication required convincing other people that one's work had merit. This constituted a check on the appetite of people for self-display. Editors and publishers exercised two central powers: they brought good work to the attention of the public and suppressed the graceless efforts of ordinary minds. The obstacle they represented was actually a vital safeguard so people would not embarrass themselves by simple ideas and inferior prose.

Today, by contrast, people can discuss their digestive difficulties on Facebook or start a blog and fill cyberspace with a torrent of words. Questionable facts, mundane experiences, incoherent reflections, and ignorant theories can be conveyed for consideration to the universe. Prejudices may be presented as considered judgments, and untutored feelings are permitted to seize the focus of attention. There seems to be no one to tell bloggers to rethink and rephrase because what they produce is a draft in need of craft. It is important to remember that even if people never had better thoughts than they have today, only a few of them ought to be preserved. The proper fate of the rest is to remain the private possession of uninteresting minds and to accompany their owners quietly to the grave.

Paradoxically, one direct outcome of the immense accumulation of knowledge made possible by mediation is the corresponding growth of ignorance. Working in large institutions, people have little idea of the complex wholes to which they contribute. It is safe to say that in an extensive chain of mediation, no one knows all the links involved. Bosses lack information about how their orders are carried out; workers have little understanding of the rules, structures, policies, and purposes of the organization; and the individuals who profit by the social acts performed have no idea how they came about. The ignorance is pervasive and proportionate to the size of the institution: the more intermediaries separate me from distant collaborators and from the results of the actions to which I contribute, the less I know about what the others do and what together we manage to bring about.

German farmers during the Second World War did not know that the food they raised sustained guards operating the gas chambers. Odd as it may sound, people in mediated chains literally do not know what they are doing. Of course, they are not blind to the motions they directly perform: they know that they plant wheat, write things down, and operate machines. But these motions are not the social act, which is vastly more complex and rich in consequences than anything a single person can do. This is why the defense "I did not know that I was party to such acts" is not trivial and not a lie. Well-meaning people sometimes learn too late that what appeared to be innocent actions on the individual level contributed to horrendous abuses in their consequences. We may argue that the people involved should have known what they were supporting, and stricter criteria of responsibility are meant to foster such broader consciousness. But the knowledge is hard to come by, and especially so if the institution (or the government) prefers secrecy.

The specialization of mediated life causes ignorance on yet another level. At a primitive stage of social development, individuals had to do pretty much everything for themselves. They had to build their own homes, hunt or raise their food, and arrange for their security. As a result, they had firsthand acquaintance with a variety of activities. Today, by contrast, we have direct knowledge of only a few sorts of actions; for everything else that may be needed, we have to call in specialists. Dispersing essential survival skills leaves us without a direct feel of the world. We may have a verbal understanding of how things operate, but we lack hands-on experience and the skill to deal with them. So even though we know far more facts than the people who preceded us, we lack the joy of experiencing life in its variety and the intelligence to master it.

There is a connection to explore here between truncated lives and the psychological problems reported by people who search in vain for meaning. Lived in its multifaceted immediacy, existence tends to be satisfying. The problems that arise engage the whole person; their solution contributes to the excitement of being alive. People can of course be overwhelmed, but to the extent that they trade blows with the world, they do not suffer from boredom and a sense of the meaninglessness of it all. They accumulate a variety of skills and learn to approach life as if they knew its secret. The knowledge is not verbal; it cannot be readily conveyed or explained, but it shapes both external responses and the internal life. It never occurs to such people to ask about the meaning of life; they are too busy leading it.

Mediation robs us of the rich variety of experiences that make life rewarding. Though we know a great deal in a distant, conceptual way, our immediacy is restricted to a relatively impoverished set of activities. Work is routinized, and repetition defines nearly everything we do. Social control over much of the world has made entire areas of life predictable. Knowledge of what is likely to happen kills spontaneity and surprise, and the sacred excitement of being alive is occluded by boredom. "Is this all there is?" becomes the central question as people wait for retirement and often death shortly after. The vaunted ideal of the Renaissance person is not to be conceived in terms of extent of knowledge but scope of skill and experience. Mediation provides us with much unimportant information at the price of surrendering full-bodied engagement with life.

11 (D) Manipulation

LARGE-SCALE MEDIATED CHAINS made it possible, the first time in history, for human beings to live in relative comfort. Coordinated labor created a surplus of goods, so at least in industrializing societies, people had enough to eat and were able to live in acceptable quarters. The idea that we have dignity and must not be abused arose on this foundation; so long as humans compete with each other for survival, we cannot expect them to treat one another with moral concern. Immanuel Kant formulated the thought that we are not to treat each other as means only and affirmed that all humans, because they were (at least potentially) rational, deserved to be handled with respect.

Kant's imperative was carefully crafted to retain the legitimacy of mediation, that is, human collaboration or the use of others as instruments of our will. If other humans could not serve as means to our ends, we would quickly regress to the level of our cave-dwelling ancestors. Therefore, Kant added the word *only* to his formula, suggesting that if we wish to attain moral standing in our activities, we must at least invite the agreement of our mediating partners. I can, for example, use pilots to get me where I want to go, so long as they want to go to the same place and don't mind taking me with them. The notion that all of us are worthy of respect underlies the grand idea of human rights and the practices of democracy. In this way, mediation provides the conditions for a humane life potentially for all, honoring humans by taking their wants and needs into full account.

Unfortunately, the mediation that makes decent life possible also fosters a fierce manipulativeness that degrades human relations. A personal story may make this point clear. Some years ago, before everybody had computers, one of our departmental secretaries and I had a particularly cordial and productive relation. I used to come to the office and smile and chat and praise her for a few minutes before asking for her help. She, in turn, would bask in the attention and then do the typing I gave her quickly and accurately before everybody else's.

The relationship was so satisfactory that I hardly noticed when at one point she started falling behind in her work, and the typing she returned showed a variety of errors. I also did not detect that her laughter had grown weak and that her eyes stayed red throughout the day. I never asked if something bothered her, and I remember being annoyed that my smile and compliments no longer brought results. I learned only later that the department's other secretary had stolen her husband and that she was going through a bitter divorce.

When I reflect on this experience, it is clear that I never took a personal interest in this person. I wanted only my writing typed and my calls placed. Our relationship was determined by the positions we held in a chain of intermediaries: I as professor and she as administrative assistant. We saw each other as occupying certain roles and not as full-fledged human beings. Her role required a cheerful face and rapid fingers; my job enabled me to use her services to get my papers out. The human connection between the two of us was submerged in a professional relationship in which there was no room for caring on my part or for showing grief on hers.

A striking feature of the interaction was our silent recognition that professional relations exclude personal elements. But we went a step further by not even noticing each other's human condition; I did not see her distress just as she probably paid no heed to my thoughtlessness. Our only interest in mediated chains is to get things done. The niceties of human interaction have in this context the single function of stimulating performance. The simulacrum of friendship and seemingly generous gestures are contrived devices to elicit the right behavior. Of praise and support not a word is meant, and often reluctant compliance with official demands hides only resentment.

Mediated chains invite manipulation, and manipulation undermines the moral structure of human interactions. The ultimate results are inability to distinguish sincere from artificial sentiments and reluctance to trust anything. The powerful desire we all have to believe in others can then be exploited by the sex-hungry, by con men, and by politicians. I once overheard a conversation between an elected official and his aide. "The most difficult thing to attain is sincerity," the politician advised. "Once you learn to fake that, you'll get elected."

In mediated chains efficiency demands the sacrifice of caring. Rules govern what we must do and what we may expect; the roles we play create and limit our power. But the power may never be used to answer human needs if they are not within the established general purposes of the chain. The rules require focus and allow no exceptions. The crushing argument for rigidity is the sentence "If we did this for you, we would have to do it for everyone." This is the ultimate self-justification of the bureaucrat, even if no other person would ever want that exception made. But variance disturbs the order of institutional life, which is thought to be at its best when it goes smoothly, that is, when it is mechanical.

In the mediated world, human needs tend to be viewed as nuisances, and the aim of social effort is manageable uniformity. This destroys the spontaneous interest of people in the welfare of their neighbors, making it easy to confuse moral life with allegiance to the system. We end as functionaries carrying out rules no one remembers making. In this way, we find justification for our questionable acts: concentration camp guards, trainmen taking people to Siberia, and even state executioners can see their work as essential to public order. Promotion and the promise of more money are used as devices of manipulation, enticing people to give themselves over to the mediated chain in which they serve.

12 (E) Psychic Distance

MEDIATION DISTANCES PEOPLE from their actions and from the consequences of what they do. The reason is that most actions in the modern world are social and cannot be performed alone. It takes thousands of people to build a car and many more to provide electricity. The interposition of agents between individuals and the acts they help to bring about obscures the nature of what they do and hides its consequences. Workers in a coal-fired power plant tend to have little knowledge of the complex interactions required to bring electricity into my home and may be altogether ignorant of the long-term problems of strip mining, acid rain, and global warming.

When actions are performed by others on my behalf, typically I have no direct experience of the act. In some important sense, the action performed for me is mine. Yet I am likely to know little of its nature and almost nothing of its consequences. As a result, I find myself abstracted from my acts. I lose contact with what is necessary to sustain my existence and express myself. Specialists do everything or almost everything for me, and I end up in isolation from my roots and leaves.

Generally, psychic distance is ignorance of the interconnectedness of social acts. Under its rubric I include several related kinds of malformation. The first is unawareness of the conditions and consequences of actions to which we contribute. Although this is ubiquitous in the modern world, it appears strange from the perspective of what I have called the complete human act. Such actions, though limited in their scope, are impossible to perform without significant knowledge of what is necessary for them and what are likely to flow from them. They include intention, execution, and consequences, along with the conditions of the act. Early hunters made their own weapons out of materials at hand whose nature they understood. They intended to employ them and knew how. Moreover, they were familiar with the consequences of their use. In large-scale social acts, by contrast, the intimacy of this integrated act is lost, and people find themselves contributing to activities that, if they understood them, they would roundly condemn.

Psychic distance increases with the number of intermediaries between agents and their acts. People at each point in the chain are specialized. Their duties are related to each other in complex ways difficult to trace. The vast majority of them are strangers to each other. What they do is alien or mysterious; sometimes people discover to their surprise that they work for the same company and on the same project. These facts make it nearly impossible for employees to appropriate the larger act as their own. This has profound implications for worker loyalty and the readiness to assume responsibility for the social act and its untoward consequences. Pride in work, understanding the vital importance of one's own contribution, and seeing coworkers as partners all suffer or are eliminated.

Further, persons submerged in large mediated chains are not likely to witness the outcomes of the social acts they help to bring about. Sometimes it is impossible not to know what a company does or manufactures; in many cases, however, employees remain ignorant of what is made, how it is sold, and why it is important to have such things on the market. And even if employees know a lot about the company, they may not realize and cannot control the uses of their products. Individuals making explosives do not know if their product will be used for blasting at construction sites or blowing up human beings. People who make cell phones can have no idea of what nefarious plans communication by means of them may make possible.

Psychic distance has a variety of sources, all connected to mediation. I have already pointed to three. Employees in mediated chains may not see how act-fragments performed by different people combine to make a whole. Those in the chain may not be familiar with the consequences of the act or the outcomes of using the products of the company. For a variety of reasons connected to mediation, members of the chain cannot consider its actions as their own. A fourth root of psychic distance is the physical remoteness of the chain's participants or products. This makes it difficult to obtain concrete knowledge of what is going on and impossible to exert effective control.

There is yet another, and more pernicious, source of psychic distance. People can learn to wrench themselves away from what is in plain view. They can see hunger and say that it is genuinely bad, yet fail to do anything about it. In this case, the problem is lack of immediate sensory experience. It is one thing to announce the evils of starvation and something altogether different to go without food for two days. Mediation tends to limit, and in some cases to eliminate, immediate experience. This is particularly dangerous because shared experience is a primary source of the solidarity of human beings. Without suffering, there is no sympathy with pain; without sad loss, words of comfort remain only words.

The success of mediation places us in a cocoon. Although we can be in touch with people on the other side of the globe, our sensory exposure to the world immediately present is sharply limited. Telephones, televisions, computers, and fax machines present us with mediated immediacies: the pictures they paint seem direct but are in fact creatures of the media. They do not put us in touch with how things are in their rich native life, but provide a selective, impoverished, and reconstructed presentation of the distant scene. I once saw a collection of friends, meeting for an evening out, all sitting at a table absorbed in their tablets and telephones. It is as if they said, "We don't need a hug and a conversation face-to-face, so long as we can text someone a thousand miles away."

There is much we cannot learn without direct experience. Nothing demonstrates this better than attending to which side of an action one happens to be on. A bomber pilot taught me the profound truth of this. He made his bombing runs with calm assurance, drinking coffee and chatting with his crew. At one point, his plane was shot down. He survived and was detained in a camp not far from where the bombs fell. He knew the sounds of his friends' planes, knew that they just had their coffee, and knew when the bombing runs began. But now he felt the immediacy of the danger and trembled as the explosions neared.

13 (F) Irresponsibility

UNDER COMMUNIST RULE, the state-employed workers of Eastern Europe became famous for their irresponsibility. Production was inefficient, the performance of duties on a job was perfunctory, and the quality of service was inferior. Few workers displayed interest in their jobs; fewer still took pride in what they did. Censure from supervisors was greeted with sullenness, complaints from customers with a shrug of the shoulders or a quiet curse. On being called on the carpet, the standard defense for incompetence or for anything that went awry was the declaration "I only work here."

This magic sentence implies that I do not make the rules and do not wish to be responsible when I apply them. It suggests that I have little notion of the interconnectedness of things and desire to restrict my operation to the narrowest limits of my job. This is one of the meanings of the word *job*. A job in this sense is contrasted with a position or membership in a profession; it is a task to be performed for pay as mechanically as possible. Individuals who hold down jobs in this sense, whether in corporations or in government, make sure that there is little personal investment in their labor. Work for them is something that must be done for a living. Their conception of it is expressed accurately by the description a telephone company employee once gave me. "It is as if I took a deep breath at eight fifteen in the morning and went under water," he said. "I surface about five o'clock in the afternoon and breathe again."

Jobs, in the current sense, are narrow roles in which virtually each operation to be performed requires explicit instructions. The human beings who perform these roles seem denuded of activity and wait like machine parts to be caused to act. Since the cause of the action, the purpose, and the motive all come from outside, it is not altogether surprising that people refuse to feel responsible for failures. Machines, after all, are mere instruments, and no one could rightly blame the car for crushing a man when the driver is drunk.

We may feel reassured that such irresponsibility occurs only under stressful circumstances in lands far away. But employers and customers alike are keenly aware that something like this is a widespread and growing reality in our country as well. Businesspeople complain vigorously about the difficulty of obtaining the services of people who are willing to work. What they mean by "someone willing to work" is someone who is self-motivated. That, in turn, involves the readiness to assume responsibility for getting things done, along with the corresponding responsibility for failure when that occurs.

Irresponsibility grows out of the inability and unwillingness of individuals to appropriate the actions to which they contribute. The actions tend to be large-scale social operations performed by corporations or government. Since the vast majority of workers do not make the plans and rules that govern their activities and for the most part do not suffer the ill effects of corporate inhumanity, they view themselves as at a distance from what they do. They think they are hired hands who can shrug their shoulders when things don't go right and disclaim responsibility by saying that they were just following orders or someone else's design. The inability to see the act as their own is understandable. In one sense at least, it is truly not theirs. But in another sense, they acquire the moral weight of it by cooperating with others to bring it about. The unwillingness to embrace responsibility for the act follows naturally: it feels unjust to be blamed for doing something one never intended and did not control.

14 Major Mediators

Tools

Humans are among the most vulnerable animals. They are born defenseless and unable to take care of themselves. Unaided, their physical power is sharply limited; they don't even enjoy the benefits of claws and fur. Without a measure of ingenuity, they would perish of the cold or of starvation. Their dependence at birth and their constant exposure to danger predisposes them to social life, which, though it demands self-control, offers protection and companionship.

To avoid frustration, suffering, and early death, humans interpose tools between themselves and what needs to be accomplished. Our ancestors used spears and stones to kill animals for food and for the warmth of their fur. Their intelligence motivated by fear, they developed clothing, protection for their feet, hatchets, projectiles, and hiding places. A tool is a physical object or event used to attain desired results. A hammer is such an object, and the song of birds is such an event. Hammers can be used to drive nails; birds use their song to attract a mate. This shows that nothing is intrinsically a tool; objects and events attain that status when they are put to use. On the operational side, therefore, people have to develop skills and habits of action that convert otherwise useless items into valuable instruments. Early humans had to learn how to throw stones, how to kill with a lance, and how to climb trees when the wounded animal attacks. Our situation is no different, except that the tools we use are more complex, and some of the skills necessary to operate them require more extensive training.

One could argue that tools are the quintessential mediators. We interpose them between ourselves and the tasks to be accomplished, sometimes to enhance security, at others to increase the range and power of our actions. We use physical objects to relieve ourselves of onerous tasks and heavy labor; properly employed, they can greatly increase the efficiency and efficacy of what the unaided body can do. The craftsman's box of tools contains a marvelous selection of devices to construct or fix whatever a properly operating house may require. The great advantage of such tools is that whoever works with them knows their power and their limits. Craftsmen enjoy immediate acquaintance with their tools; they know what they are good for and what cannot be expected of them. As a result, control remains in the hands of the worker, and surprises are relatively rare.

Cheerleaders for humanity boldly assert that we are "the tool-using animal." No other species is supposed to have the rationality to convert desires into goal-directed action; the fact that we can presumably provides added reason for supposing that we are the crown of creation. Such myths thrive on inattention. Most of us don't watch and don't notice what animals do. Purposive activity is present nearly everywhere in the animal kingdom, from chipmunks collecting corn for the winter to birds building their nests out of leaves and branches.

Never have I seen animal use of tools more clearly than one striking afternoon in the London Zoo. Children were throwing fruit and candy to a gorilla, with many of them falling short of the cage. The gorilla took a stout branch off a tree, cleaned it of leaves, and began using it to bring the sweets closer to his body. He evidently enjoyed the food, but to get more he soon had to stretch ever farther, until he could no longer command the stick and it fell on the ground beyond his reach. He stood puzzled, trying to assess the situation. There was no other long branch to remove from the tree. Instead, he found a crooked, short branch, which he took, cleaned, and used to coax the original stick close enough to pick up from his cage. I was astonished that he not only used a tool but also understood how to employ a tool to gain access to another one.

Individual workers operating with simple tools find mediation unproblematic. They welcome the opportunity to protect themselves and expand the sphere of their agency. Passivity, a sense of impotence, and psychic distance, along with the other costs of mediation, are absent at this stage and appear only when tools become complex and can no longer be wielded by one or a few skilled individuals. The development of ever more complicated and powerful tools requires a corresponding growth of skills and social collaboration. It doesn't take much to make a hammer and to learn its virtues. But no one can make a plane, and even pilots who know how to fly them have little understanding of the parts and operations of the engines. To create and use such complex tools, large numbers of specialized workers must cooperate, and the sheer number of such agents makes their ignorance of each others' work difficult to avoid.

To be sure that complex tools remain operable, work with them has to be simplified. Electric generation plants are designed so that a few buttons and levers control vast and vastly complex processes, and the assembly line has become famous for the repetitious but crushingly simple movements necessary for efficiency. Simplicity is gained at the price of blinding ignorance and the sense of not being in control, which culminate in unwillingness to take responsibility. These are the costs of mediation, while lives of comfort and relative security constitute its benefits.

The arrival of computers and other electronic devices signaled a new chapter in the development of tools. In certain respects, they function as inanimate brains, aiding us in the tasks of calculating, integrating, and remembering. They can store and retrieve prodigious amounts of information, communicate with each other and with humans from a great distance, and even offer rudimentary judgments. The further development of these tools is unpredictable; all we know is that it will be full of surprises. In one of their applications, they can keep tabs on how humans behave, sending tickets, for example, automatically to whomever their speed sensors detect. Because they are precise and unforgiving, they constitute a greater threat to freedom than humans do. No other tool can match the danger to privacy they represent: they can spy on people and accumulate mounds of information about them. Grocery stores photograph the movements of customers and monitor their purchases. For commercial or for no particular purpose, companies invade private computers and gather and keep data concerning search habits.

To top it all, government agencies record the communications of people with each other, along with their feelings, opinions, and tastes. When corporations meddle in people's affairs, the reaction is annoyance, but when governments do so, intimidation becomes a factor. In East Germany during the communist era, rumor had it that one-third of the population spied on the remaining two-thirds. There, however, people could at least whisper their convictions to their spouses in the quiet of their bedrooms. In today's world, not even the bedroom is safe: telephones and tablets can be turned on from a distance and made to serve as listening devices, and computers with virtually endless storage capacity are ready to record whatever anyone believes.

In prior ages, things happened and lives were led only to be mercifully forgotten. Forgetfulness appears to be a luxury we can no longer afford. Everything is recorded and kept for a posterity unlikely to be interested. Like a retentive patient, we hold on to information as if it mattered; we cannot let go of it for fear that we might miss something. We justify the illness in terms of the need for research or national security, but in reality we are propelled by the love of gossip: we want to know everything about everybody.

In its early development, humankind turned to tools to improve its lot. The tools were not sophisticated enough to wrest control from their creators. The growth of technology changed the balance of power: instead of being their helpmate, in certain respects technology turned humans into appendages of machines. Its wholesome effects are offset by the costs of its mediating function. We could probably not live without our machines, but we pay an ever increasing price for the comfort they provide.

15 Major Mediators

Language

In what we call "civilized" countries, people swim in a sea of talk. Discussing things is considered a sign of education, refinement, or even moral excellence. The right words are supposed to be capable of rearranging the world, establishing purposes, creating alliances to accomplish them, and making sure that what is achieved remains a part of the permanent good. People believe that the magical power of what we say supplants the need for warfare, and conversation—if only it could go on long enough—would demonstrate that the interests of feuding parties converge. A tsunami of talk is supposed to sweep away all disagreement and resolve even the bitterest conflicts.

Convictions of this sort have been shown to be naive again and again. Value commitments are often divergent and sometimes incompatible. Agreement must be built on shared beliefs about the good; if some treasure life, but others, motivated by hatred, are willing to give up even their own, peaceful coexistence becomes impossible. Such irresolvable conflicts show the impotence of talk or its function as a ruse: people propelled by religion or ideology talk only to disguise their preparations to fight. Of course, doubts about the universal efficacy of language must not be taken as denials of its remarkable power. Speech that engages the emotions can lead to violent action, and vicious rumors widely circulated leave reputations in shambles. An appreciation of what language can and what it cannot do helps us understand its ambiguous role as both a prime instrument of mediation and a means of overcoming some of the harmful effects of psychic distance.

Often, talk takes the place of direct experience. We tend to seek descriptions and explanations that can be provided only in language, overlooking the fact that immediate encounter with the world is a more powerful and more reliable guide to life. The German philosopher Arthur Schopenhauer was right in saying that both animals and humans grasp causal connections intuitively. No linguistic account is needed to explain the connection between a blow to the head and collapsing on the floor. Even dogs know to run from the stick wielded by someone angry; all they need is a bit of past experience and a glance at the situation. Many animals operate successfully without words of clarification, and so do humans when they attend to the task at hand. Surgeons do not chatter when they make incisions, and performance is rarely enhanced by explanations in the act of love. We may no longer live in the bosom of nature, but nature continues to live in our bosom, and through action we find ourselves in deep harmony with the world.

Groucho Marx gave memorable performances of the buffoon who substitutes talk for what needs to be done. In our crowded world, all of us have to do this to some extent, sharing ideas and experiences through the medium of language. The plenitude of words reveals the experience, but only at a distance. To be sure, we enjoy some direct contact, but for the most part only with sentences and words, and they stand in the way of the immediacy they are supposed to convey. The infatuation with language is best demonstrated by a couple I once saw not looking up from their guidebooks to see Niagara Falls.

The immediacy that comes of sensory exposure cannot be conveyed; we can only live and experience it. Words as substitutes for experience accomplish two functions that pull in different directions. They offer the advantage of learning about the richness of distant realities, making it unnecessary to travel the Silk Road and visit Samarkand. In this way, the library becomes the world, and we create a thin, romantic image of what is beyond our senses. This picture gallery provides readers with ideas about how others feel and live. Of course, the information is partial and inadequate, and, even in the hands of the best storytellers and writers, it lacks the vibrancy of being there. But at least it expands the sphere of our acquaintance and adds a little to the stock of our knowledge.

On the other hand, language often stands as a barrier to experience. Its pliant efficacy suggests that direct acquaintance adds little or nothing to our lives. And indeed, we think that so long as we speak, hear, write, and read enough, we have no need of pesky exposure to the world. But without the color, taste, and smell of what surrounds us, we live impoverished lives. Good writing can stimulate the imagination and evoke empathy, but the power of words is as nothing by comparison with direct perception of the pain of others. Once again, Schopenhauer was right that, in suffering, we are united with all sentient creatures. Language undercuts this unity and immediacy by the impertinence of trying to describe the private struggles of the soul.

My intention is not to denigrate language or to deny its importance. We need to acknowledge its value in making large-scale human communication possible. Yet we must also call attention to its mediating functions and the costs they incur. Language enables us to achieve conceptual clarity and transcend distances of space and time. However, it also stands between us as an alien medium. It turns our minds away from direct contact with our neighbors, building walls of words to protect from the impact of life and to hide our deepest feelings. In the face of tender human relations, language remains speechless. Its limit is the sigh or silence of lovers, the hug of reunion, and the endless grief over a child who will never return.

16 Major Mediators
Ideology

To MANY, IDEOLOGIES represent welcome relief from the confusions of thought. Understanding what happens is difficult; it requires sound judgment and considerable knowledge of the world. One must learn to be skeptical, and questioning plausible claims goes against the grain. The American philosopher Charles Sanders Peirce speaks of doubt as an irritant; people seek comfort and come to rest frequently in the first idea they can believe. As a result, from time to time, we meet persons whose minds are populated by bizarre notions. They think, we are wont to say, as if they were from another planet, embracing views of the world that seem to have only the feeblest connection to reality.

The deepest conviction or at least hope of people is that there is a single truth about everything in the world. Any opinion that does not capitulate to this truth must be simply false and, as such, unworthy of belief. The notion that there may be as much to say for any view as there is for its opposite is disquieting and feels like surrender of the quest for truth. The idea that we live in a world of probabilities is alien to most of us and difficult to grasp. The weather forecast that promises a 20 percent chance of rain seems to offer gibberish: we think we know that either it will rain or it won't, and that is the end of the matter. To say that it may or may not is but a confession of ignorance and not an assessment of the objective situation. We tend to think that action requires unquestionable information and refuse to believe that everywhere we turn life faces uncertainty.

This determined search for truth, knowledge, and above all assurance prepares the mind for ideology, a relatively simple set of ideas that explains everything. Frequently, ideology arrives with an announcement of conspiracy. The truth is within reach, it promises, but nefarious interests deny us access to it. These wicked influences emanate from the devil or from false consciousness induced by capitalism. They may derive from forces seeking to dominate us or, as I once read in a handbill in London, from the unholy team of the Pope and the Queen of England. The claim of conspiracy makes the ideology vibrantly attractive, offering us the benefits of revelation or at least the excitement of coming out of darkness into light.

The ideology itself may range from the simple affirmation of a hierarchy, as in the belief that some races or religions are superior to others, to the complex simulacrum of scientific thought, as is presented in Marxism. The ideological claims tend to be sweeping and universal in the sense of accounting for everything. The inferiority of a race or of some social or economic arrangement offers an understanding of all that ails us and invites obliteration of this well of evil. In this way, ideology both enlightens and purifies: it presents a diagnosis of our ills and outlines what we must do to attain utopia. It permits no uncertainty and no hesitation. The call to action is absolute, and backsliders are banished from the ranks of true believers.

As a way of thinking, ideology becomes a mediating force structuring the relations of human beings. Its followers find it difficult to view people as living and suffering individuals. Instead, they think of them as instances of stereotypes—that is, as women, Jews, blacks, infidels, or capitalists. This destroys the human kinship between oneself and others, displaying whoever does not agree with the ruling way of thought as blind and alien. Sorting people through the categories of ideology makes it acceptable to treat them as members of a group, most often a despised group, and to disregard their personal characteristics. But to reduce the complex reality of human beings to membership in a class is to strip them of everything that makes them special. We end unable to approach one another as individuals every one of whom is, in important respects, an exception.

Ideological convictions have been the source of profound dehumanization. They tend to separate the population of the world into "them" and "us," assigning purity and virtue to those who believe and evil intentions to everyone else. Our nature harbors tensions and contradictions. The spontaneous fashion in which feelings of joy and grief can spread is offset by the difficulty of placing ourselves in the shoes of others. The cruelties visited upon "them" are best explained by the fact that ideology makes us view people as objects to be swept away and not as suffering human beings. To be unmoved by the pleas of living persons is to view them as emptied of their humanity and having no claim on us.

The simplifying power of ideology is magical. We are saved the need to think; everything worth knowing has already been determined by leaders who know better. All we need to do is repeat the powerful slogans. Continuous incantations heap added certainty on the ideas, and resistance to them only proves their truth and the self-seeking wickedness of the opposition. When ideology invades our view of the world, we lose precious immediacy with each other. We then think we can escape the uncertainties of existence and dispense with the struggle for a better life.

17 Major Mediators

Institutions

Institutions may constitute the most remarkable achievement of the human race. They are patterns of the interactions of people designed to attain ends otherwise beyond our reach. Contrary to the claims of those who think that institutions are independently existing super-organisms, they are best understood as consisting of the cooperative actions of individuals. The level of collaboration required to sustain a well-functioning institution was beyond anything conceivable to our distant ancestors. They repeated their actions by habit, and sometimes the habits intersected, but cooperation was occasional and neither planned nor sustained. If we compare their efforts with the tight interconnections of the actions of a hundred thousand individuals employed by an international bank, we begin to see how far we have progressed.

The work of most people in institutions is routine and repetitious. They perform a repertory of similar actions, adding minor but perhaps indispensable contributions to the outcome. The achievement, such as the erection of skyscrapers, belongs to everyone who made it possible. The tasks of both those who plan and those who execute the plans are carefully orchestrated, with written and unwritten rules governing what is to be done, when, and how. The coordination requires that the actions mandated by the institution take precedence over what one would like to do if one were left alone—workers cannot take a walk and smoke cigarettes when the beams that hold the building are to be installed. In this way, institutions exercise a profoundly civilizing influence over individuals. They nullify the pull of self-willed actions by requiring that their employees do what conduces to the benefit of the company.

Institutions thus perform a moral function without aiming to do so and often without knowing it. At their best, they harness the self-interested energies of people and apply them to tasks that help others live and live well. Of course, institutions can also be destructive, aiming at mischief and even the extermination of groups of people. But the vast majority of organizations, especially in a well-functioning commercial society, operate on the principle that the good of the individual and the good of the community converge. To flourish, people have to hold down jobs, and the employment provided by institutions guides them to perform socially useful acts. Unfortunately, the vast benefits institutions secure are easily forgotten, and people who like to do what they want and not what they must come to view them as alien and oppressive structures. Even some of their champions tend to overlook the good they do and try to justify them as necessary evils.

The positive function of institutions must not go unmentioned before we assess the costs of their operation. Life without them would be miserable, perhaps hardly possible. But a world of large institutions also presents serious problems for individuals. The primary cause of the difficulties is the size of the mediated chains of which institutions consist. In a small organization, the participants inevitably get to know one another: each person is both a functioning link and a living being with special needs. Direct acquaintance with others and the necessity to accommodate them gives everyone the sense that they have *standing*, which is the reasonable expectation that their ideas and desires are taken into account—that is, that they matter.

In large, impersonal institutions, this standing disappears. Individuals are reduced to the functions they perform, and the care and consideration they receive are identical to what others in a similar position obtain. The principle that each individual is an exception and may require special treatment is rejected in favor of general rules that presumably advance the interests of the organization and, through them, the good of its members. Naturally, people whose ideas and desires are disregarded find themselves at odds with the organization. They see the rules as amounting to a callous disregard of their special needs and unique situation. They seek differential treatment or some relief from the established norms or, at the very least, acknowledgment that a variance would be appropriate.

To their endless frustration, however, individuals are greeted by the senseless and insensitive "If we did this for you, we would have to do it for everyone." As an attempt to impose the universal on the particular, this is experienced as a flimsy excuse for doing nothing. We all know that not everyone is in a similar situation, and not everyone demands a variance. The result is the sense that, as employees or customers, we are replaceable ciphers whose feelings are irrelevant. Huge institutions keep us strangers, or worse, faceless numbers to process. The humane aspect of our interactions disappears in the bureaucracy, and we unlearn the principles, which it took thousands of years to establish, of what not to do to our neighbors.

This bureaucratization of highly populous societies leads naturally to depersonalized human relations. When everyone receives the same treatment, no one can stand out as deserving special consideration. From the standpoint of the orchestra, musicians must play their parts without complaint. Yet each plays a solo instrument that opens unique possibilities and imposes special needs. Embracing the kind of odd contradiction he favored, Hegel maintained that in being a different individual, every person is the same. Each of us is unique and therefore just like everyone else. This means, of course, that no one is worthy of special consideration. The key distinction, he thought, is between the multitude of ordinary individuals, who are born and pass away, and the universal individual that all persons embody while it remains unchanged.

Although this is a distinction one can make, it has no bearing on the proper treatment of human beings. Declaring that if *everyone* is unique, no one really is, misses the central point about persons. They are worlds unto themselves, each consisting of emotions, judgments, values, and experiences that can be understood only from their own perspective.[1] The abstract statement that everyone is unique does not capture anyone's mode of uniqueness; striking peculiarities distinguish us, and the differences overwhelm our similarities.

Rules define the roles we fill in institutions. The size and structure of organizations make it difficult to know much more than what one's role demands, and functionaries try to avoid responsibility for their actions by hiding behind narrow readings of their job descriptions. Nazi guards at death camps maintained that they were simply following orders, and Soviet trainmen taking deportees to Siberia, never to return, insisted that they were simply providing transportation. Even in a benign system, inhumanity is difficult to avoid, because people who could make a difference refuse to take personal responsibility for their acts.

Only on rare occasions is there in institutions a meeting of humans unmediated by the rules of the organization and the roles played by its employees. Face-to-face immediacy enables people to appreciate each other's predicaments; without it, the capacity for empathy is disengaged, and communication remains shallow. Sales organizations, endorsing such principles as "The customer is always right," attempt to overcome bureaucratic indifference or sluggishness, but even an earnest effort at humanizing the institution is likely to fail. We come up here against the very nature of large organizations whose mediated chains of employees cannot be taught to act as though they cared.

People who have dealt with large institutions (and all of us have) are likely to remember their maddening inhumanity. They do not mean to frustrate us; on the contrary, their motto is service, and their intentions are, for the most part, benign. But to fulfill their purposes, they need order and predictability, and those cannot be attained without firm rules and uniform procedures. The rules, in turn, tend to freeze into rigid behaviors that favor the efficiency of the organization instead of its receptivity. The aim to serve the community is then replaced by the drive to succeed, which ultimately yields its place to the desperate goal of survival.

The losers are the customers or clients who telephone in to have an error rectified and find themselves talking to a machine. A human being would understand the problem and take remedial action, but the machine works with inflexible categories and permits no deviation or explanation. In such a world, even getting a living soul on the line is an achievement. When at last an operator checks in, it is crushing to realize that we have made little headway: in their official roles, humans often act like machines. Much as specialists in public relations remind employees to be respectful and kind, in large organizations the ignorance and irresponsibility of the mediated world take over and convert our comfort into misery.

Note

1. See my "Subjective Worlds," *Review of Metaphysics* 66 (June 2013): 809–21.

18 Major Mediators

Government

SOME PEOPLE THINK that the current division of the world into nation-states is artificial and immoral. Human groups, they believe, should not be separated in ways that make conflict among them likely and perhaps inevitable. The resources of the earth belong to everyone, so their uneven distribution enforced by patrolled borders and restrictive immigration laws is ethically unacceptable. People who think this way look forward to a time when nation-states disappear and a cosmopolitan world order takes their place.

This is a bold, and in some respects attractive, hope. But in assessing its value, it is important to keep in mind that the development of nation-states represented a great advance over living under the arbitrary rule of local warlords. Central governments made due process and uniform treatment of individuals at least possible. They also offered protection of life and property, conducing to a measure of social order. In addition, the development of a variety of languages, cultures, and literatures constitutes a significant enrichment of the human spirit. So the disappearance of nation-states would not be a costless benefit. In fact, it may lead to the destruction of many ways of life, along with the cultures that support them. The victory of McDonald's over local restaurants in Moscow and Hong Kong is not pleasant to contemplate.

Although a borderless world may bring about some desirable outcomes, the reduction of mediation is not one of them. In fact, a single huge governmental structure is likely to make some forms of alienation more severe than anything we have seen before. The governments of populous states consist of armies of politicians and civil servants, interconnected in complex and, to outsiders, opaque ways. The ill effects of mediation are proportional to the size of the chains of functionaries that operate our institutions. Commercial organizations employ hundreds of thousands of people who, along with their customers, suffer from significant psychic distance and irresponsibility. The governments of large nations encompass millions of people, most of whom have at best a sketchy idea of how what they do connects to the work of others.

In the United States, even presidents are unlikely to have a clear idea of all the agencies that act on their behalf. Even if they memorized all that government does and mastered the details of their lines of authority, they could not control their behavior. The longer the mediated chains, the less the center can control the agents on the periphery. There are always reasons why things can't be done the way the boss wants and explanations why anyone not in *these* trenches cannot really see what is needed. Congressional intent evaporates on the way down to the people who have to enforce it. Creative interpretation, misunderstanding, indifference, and policy disagreements convert edicts into suggestions easy to disregard.

In commercial institutions, clients have at least a little control over the behavior of employees: the need to compete for business limits the amount of nastiness and incompetence permissible. Government, by contrast, has no competition and enjoys a monopoly of power, so citizens have no remedy against its malfeasance except what it expressly permits. In the England of the Middle Ages, the king visited each province to hear grievances that could otherwise not be resolved. Access to a just and attentive power was a vast relief to people who thought they had been wronged. Judges today rarely play this role. Their hands are tied by statute and precedent, and they don't normally have the option to overlook in the name of mercy what technically remains a crime.

The result is that government, the very agency designed to protect people, leaves people unprotected from itself. It can be sued only with its consent, and for ordinary citizens it is nearly impossible to challenge, much less change, its methods of operation. The French philosopher Jean-Jacques Rousseau proposed what he called "periodic assemblies of the people" to assess the level of satisfaction citizens experience with their servant, the government. Should the majority decide that things are not going well, the politicians could be fired on the spot. Although this may make for some instability, fear of summary dismissal might well enhance efforts to serve and to do so with a human face. In our society, we have to wait for the next election cycle for a change of leadership. And even then, entrenched civil servants are difficult to remove, and the next wave of politicians washes ashore with debts to their donors and partisan allegiances.

Language, even when truthful, tends to place itself between people and reality. When it is laden with lies, we pay the terrible price of operating with a distorted picture of the facts. Sometimes this is the result of the political life of a nation. The felt invulnerability of politicians makes it possible for them to play fast and loose with the truth. Dissemblance, vagueness, studied ambiguity, hidden agendas, willful misinterpretation, and outright deception constitute a good deal of the public discourse of nations. It would be of great value if the words of politicians were reliable mediators, that is, if citizens could operate with the sure knowledge that civil servants and elected representatives scrupulously adhered to the truth. This would require that political statements be assigned probability values: some would be presented as most likely true, others as plausible, and many as speculative, uncertain, or false.

Is it possible to reach this minor utopia? It is unreasonable to hope for the moral transformation of office seekers and office holders. We could, however, use their self-interest as ground and establish a committee to supervise political discourse. The committee would have to be tough minded and nonpartisan. It would conduct a running examination of what politicians say and publicize potential infractions. No more than three assertions of certifiable falsehoods might be allowed; upon the third, office holders would lose their offices, and they, along with aspirants, would be barred from seeking and holding elective and appointed office for a period of time.

I know that such a measure may appear excessive, and the will to enforce it may be missing. Partisans may infiltrate the committee and frustrate its purpose. All manner of obstacles may be put in the way of its proper operation. Cynics may ask what, after all, would politics be without lying. But, in spite of these and countless other objections, instituting some such control mechanism may bring home to citizens the sanctity of public conversation. What politicians tend to is the good of all, that is, the health and welfare of the entire community. To lie about that is to deny choice to citizens and to endanger their future.

A major difficulty in the way of correcting errors and reversing injustices is the tendency of bureaucracies to close ranks when under pressure. Citizen complaints are interpreted as attacks on functionaries or on the system as a whole, which engenders a bunker mentality and efforts at retaliation. The perpetrators become impossible to reach; attempts to hold them accountable or at least to change their behavior generate antagonism. A rigid defensiveness replaces the desire for humble service, and even people with legitimate complaints are tarred as troublemakers. At this point, all the ill effects of large-scale mediation come into view. Citizens feel impotent and at a psychic distance from people who act on their behalf. Civil servants become unresponsive and irresponsible; they reject the power of official discretion and permit rules and roles to define their actions. Each side begins to manipulate the other, and everyone feels free to mislead in order to get its way.

Some people employed by municipal, state, and federal governments make extraordinary efforts to serve well. They take circumstances into account and treat humans in a humane fashion. But the pressure of numbers makes it attractive to process people as if they were things and not individuals with intense personal lives. Imaginative extension of oneself into the place of another is the heart of morality, and it is precisely this achievement that, in a bureaucracy, takes extraordinary effort. Functionaries may think that they do enough if they treat each person like every other. This, however, is just the beginning of ethics. Its ultimate demand is to deal with people in their unique individuality. To those who object that this is inefficient, we can say that efficiency may be a good measure in building cars and distributing watermelons, but it is largely irrelevant when it comes to relating to fellow human beings.

In light of the cumbersome ineffectiveness of government, the ever-renewed call for reducing its size falls on fertile ground. This ideal is, however, unlikely to be realized. Civil service jobs are among the safest one can get: they are protected by public service unions and the carefully fostered impression that many social functions can be performed only by central agency. The result is a proliferation of activities more than a few of which are guided by ill-defined purposes and uncertain authority vying for growing shares of taxpayer money.

Mediated chains derive their problems from the ignorance that besets each of their elements. When chains intersect, the ignorance is vastly increased, and the workers in any one tend not to learn who else makes common cause with them. The indirection and confusion eventually become endemic, revealing that no one is in charge. Government is more like a profusion of natural growths than an expertly designed rational system.

19 Mediated Immediacies

IMAGINE A CAT living in a house and never allowed out. The house has many windows, and the cat can roam freely from one to another. The yard teems with chipmunks, squirrels, and birds, and the cat's tail twitches as it observes them. It is ready to leap to capture one or another, but of course the panes of glass that separate it from the outside world make action of that sort impossible. It can see clearly, but something essential to a full life is missing: the cat is all sight and no spring. The mediating action of the glass makes vision possible but forestalls the chase.

The cat's world is similar to some forms of virtual reality: it is splendidly vivid in certain respects and severely inadequate in others. The cat has only a simulacrum of life experience. It knows nothing of leaping on a live animal, breaking its neck with a shake, and dining on its warm body. The point is not that this is just as well. The world is a cruel place, and little is lost if cats don't go hunting. And yet, from the standpoint of the cat, a great deal is denied it. The vision is for the hunt, and the hunt is to live and flourish. Vision is no substitute for life; although it yields a kind of direct contact, the immediacy it makes available is impoverished.

There have been stunning advances creating immediacy with the hidden and the distant in the last hundred years. Not long ago, what was beyond sight could be represented only through the mediation of words: newspapers and personal reports exhausted the avenues available for learning about faraway events. The invention of the telephone and the telegraph only speeded things up without offering a new medium of communication. The development of photography, on the other hand, ushered in a new world, not mediated by words, of rapidly expanding access to the hidden corners of the earth. Television rendered this access nearly instantaneous and gave people in their living rooms the impression that they were witnessing joy and catastrophe firsthand.

The world wide web accelerated, expanded, and deepened these tendencies. With telephones that also serve as cameras and with multipurpose tablets, anyone can record and broadcast to the world some small segment of history. And what we capture are small segments indeed, but ones that present themselves as authentic and immediate. Because the eyes are engaged, no interpretation seems needed: it appears to be all there in the raw reality of it. We can feel as though we participated in the lives of Japanese tsunami victims, Ukrainian protesters, and the unfortunates whose homes were razed by last night's tornado. Distance appears to melt away, and we gain the impression that we know and understand it all.

What can be wrong with such relatively inexpensive ways of providing what feels like immediacy? Breaking down the barriers of space and time gives our minds broader scope and enables us to sympathize with suffering others. Evening news broadcasts on television, presenting vivid images of war, were supposed to have played a central role in bringing the Vietnam conflict to an end. Accuracy of this claim apart, there is little doubt that what we see through communications media engages the moral imagination: seeing the horror may not lead to action, but at the least it makes us think that something should be done.

What we might call "secondhand immediacy" has rescued us from the fate of medieval villages that served as their own little worlds and offered scant knowledge of what lay beyond. At least as far as information goes, social media move us in the direction of a global society where everyone can know everything relevant. But mediated immediacy is intrinsically selective and therefore deceptive. Because it appears to be direct experience, it blinds us to the instrumentalities involved. Like the cat that can see but not act, we are limited to a mediated, that is constructed, version of reality, a version that pretends to be more than what it is.

Immediate sensory experience comes in a context and engages the entire body. Someone jumping out of the bushes to scare a passerby evokes much more than surprise: emotions are mobilized, adrenaline flows freely, the muscles stiffen, blood pressure shoots up, the eyes dart looking for another attack, and a quick judgment is made whether to flee or fight. Having this experience is strikingly different from seeing the experience take place: the bodily reaction of an observer at a safe distance doesn't even approximate the raw scare of the person involved. To make the experience more vivid, the TV commentator *explains*, using cool words to replicate the hot experience. Whoever hasn't been exposed to both the sensory shock and the visual replica of it simply cannot assess their dissimilarities. Cats do not know what they miss when they only look.

Mediated immediacy presents reality at a great loss. This loss comes from the lack of physical and emotional involvement in the affairs of the world. A transcendental spirit might view reality this way, but such detached minds are unlikely to understand our quandaries. Mediated immediacy is therefore incapable of providing the rich experience necessary for counteracting the harmful effects of mediation. It goes a little distance toward showing what the world is like, but its world is not the one in which we act and often fail.

There is one other kind of constructed immediacy to consider. This one has little to be said for it because it provides false and misleading experiences. Television and social media offer a distorted picture of the world, but at least they deal with reality. The world of actors and actresses and politicians and celebrities is all constructed—it has nearly nothing to do with underlying reality. Many of the heavenly women of Hollywood are creatures of Botox and rouge; their world appears to be an imaginary island untouched by any of the cares of life. They reinforce the image by giving awards to each other, just as politicians heap praise on one another to establish legitimacy. Television and slick magazines are the media used to create these images, to counteract the failure and humiliation that beset them, as they beset the rest of us, in daily life.

20 Eliminate Mediation?

IF MEDIATION HAS so many harmful side effects, would it not be better simply to eliminate it? Such a course may seem particularly attractive if we consider that, for tens of thousands of years in the life of our species, mediation remained at a minimum. To be sure, there was always some social life in the process of which people did things for each other. Children needed to be fed and cared for, hunting required cooperation, and defense grew in effectiveness in proportion to the number of experienced and willing fighters. But for tens of thousands of years, there was no central government, and there were no institutions of size. People lived in small groups and managed to get by without noxious rules and external aid.

Something like this may well have been the condition of the human race at some point in the distant past. But we must be careful not to glorify such a life; people today would consider it intolerable. Without mediation, the supply of food would be uncertain and frequently interrupted. We would live in constant fear of being attacked and killed, learning by bitter experience that it is not the strong and the crafty but the stressed insomniac who survives. Travel would be nearly impossible, and even clean water would be a rare luxury. Pleasures would be brief, crude, and surrounded by anxiety and restless vigilance.

Humans constitute the only species on earth with a system of health care. When deer slip and fall, others stand around for a little while and then depart. Even gorillas cannot do much more than sympathize with the ill or hurt among them. Humans, by contrast, learn and remember what alleviates disease. This is impossible without the accumulation of knowledge and a systematic way of handing it down. Language, designated by the American philosopher John Dewey as "the tool of tools," serves as the medium that makes such cultural developments possible. As a tool, it is a powerful mediating force, both separating and uniting human beings as they tackle the tasks of life. All of this and a great deal more would be lost if we were to try to live without mediation altogether.

Of course, it is highly doubtful that this could be accomplished at all: without the use of language and other tools, human life would be but a brief planetary interlude. Hunger, inclement weather, brutal conflict, and the limited capacities of individuals would contribute to the quick extinction of the race.

Even a far less radical cutback of mediation would make daily existence awful. Some years ago, well-meaning people began to agitate for something they called "Buddhist economics," declaring that "small is beautiful." The idea was for us to live in little communities and for these villages to achieve as great a level of self-sufficiency as possible. Romantic descriptions were offered of the beauty and satisfactions of a more rural and less consumption-oriented society. The advocates of the view did all they could to shame us into what they thought were virtue and purity. And indeed, many people found these ideas attractive, even exhilarating, although few were motivated to live by them.

By a splendid self-contradiction, the people who favored reducing mediation did so while enjoying its benefits. They called for the simplification of life from the complex comforts of big cities. To make their points, they utilized national and international book publishers. They flew from city to city to appear on television shows to explain their ideas. They ate Norwegian salmon, drank Russian vodka, and maintained the comfort of their homes with oil from the Middle East. Would they have embraced simplification as the solution to our problems if they had tried it? Imagine a world without today's open flow of goods and services. Electricity, made possible by moving coal, oil, and natural gas over vast distances, would be the first casualty. Without it, cities would be plunged into darkness. Trucks and cars, requiring the mediated labor of tens of thousands of people, would no longer be manufactured and without gasoline could no longer be driven. Highways could not be maintained and would soon crumble. Communication over distances would become impossible, food would be limited to the meager variety a small village could produce, and medical care would be reduced to the administration of local herbal remedies.

We know that such societies have existed, and we have reason to believe that in their original historical appearance, not many people thought them splendid. This is the way people lived in the Middle Ages, in small communities isolated from each other and woefully impoverished. Since people then knew no better, their suffering might have been less intense than ours would be. Part of the reason for this is that they believed their condition was natural and unavoidable, but we know that things don't have to be that way. With mediation gone, we would remember that we had given up a world that, by comparison, was paradise.

Everything considered, therefore, mediation appears to be too central a part of our lives and too valuable to surrender. This, in turn, means that large organizations and big government are here to stay. The least cutback of our comfort, such as interruption of electrical service as a result of a storm, elicits loud complaints, and it would indeed be lamentable to return life to the privations faced by prior generations. This of course means that we inherit the costs of our comfort and end up suffering misery as the price of happiness. The best we can hope to do is counteract the ill effects of mediation by reducing the passivity, inhumanity, and irresponsibility it generates. If we succeed at this task, human life is likely to become significantly better.

21 Ineffective Ways of Dealing with Mediation

Even if it were possible to eliminate mediation, doing so would be too costly. We enjoy our comforts; without them, life would be bleak. A look at such major mediators as institutions and language makes it clear that even a significant reduction of mediation is unwise to attempt and, short of a nuclear catastrophe, is unlikely to occur. This leaves us with only one strategy: we must find ways to reduce the undesirable consequences of mediation. Unfortunately, this is by no means easy, because its satisfactions and its disagreeable outcomes are organically intertwined.

Before discussing effective ways of reducing the harmful psychological and social effects of mediation, we need to dispose of two wrongheaded theories of the causes and cures of our problems. The first maintains that the source of misery resides in the loss of traditional values. In earlier ages, the argument goes, people cared for each other. Living in tight-knit communities, they shared wholesome values and helped one another whenever the need arose. The secularization of society and the corrosive influence of relativism destroyed this social consensus, replacing it with crude selfishness. No surprise, then, that manipulation and irresponsibility have become natural patterns of life and everyone feels exploited and alienated. If this is the correct diagnosis of our ills, the medicine is obvious: we must cement our bonds by returning to the values of the past.

Such views have little to offer beyond nostalgia, and, as all nostalgic cravings do, they want to take us back to a sentimental but fictive past. We have reason to believe that there never was a time of general agreement concerning how to live well. If some society came close to universal compliance with its rules, its principles were likely coerced and not spontaneous. Wholehearted embrace of a few values may characterize isolated small communities, but the citizens of populous societies always pull in a number of different directions. Perhaps people cared more for each other in a distant past than we do today, but the values grounding that concern cannot be transplanted like a forsythia bush. In any case, the breakdown of traditional ways of life explains much less of the details of our comforts and discomforts than does an analysis in terms of the growth of mediation. Social agreement does not simply shrivel or disappear; its disintegration is much more likely to be the effect rather than the cause of profound social changes.

The second mistaken theory turns on the idea of false consciousness. According to this view, capitalism or some other wicked social process has so befuddled us that we have become unable to see our true condition. We don't recognize that we are unhappy, alienated, misled, duped, exploited, and confused. The very fact that we feel good confirms our ignorance; all of life in our society is a colossal show of unreality sponsored by the rich and the powerful. Satisfaction with our condition makes the lie complete: our rulers offer the cheap pleasures of consumption to suppress the deeper reaches of our nature. Manipulativeness, irresponsibility, psychic distance, and a sense of impotence are supposed to be derivable from the distorted worldview (sometimes referred to as "the inverted world") that has penetrated our consciousness. According to this picture, it will take a revolution to clear our heads and make us recognize that though we thought we were happy, we were in fact duped and always suffering.

A theory that denounces all of our ideas as false is immediately suspect. Surely, there must be a measure of truth to them, given the fact that they have helped us negotiate some treacherous turns in life. False-consciousness theories maintain that we cannot determine the truth of sociopolitical ideas until action in accordance with them brings about significant changes in us. Actions are, indeed, indispensable for the confirmation of theories, but the false-consciousness gambit confers a wrong priority on them. It is irrational to act on a view for which we have little or no evidence, maintaining that our actions might provide retrospective reasons for having done so. The claim that everything we think is wrong and everything we like is worthless makes us wonder if it may not be our revolutionaries who pull the wool over our eyes rather than our leaders. At any rate, if the illusion created is so powerful, we can rightly ask how the prophets of false consciousness managed to escape its clutches.

At a minimum, we know that ameliorative actions based on these two theories simply do not work. A few individuals who regain the faith of their mothers and fathers manage to find satisfaction for a while. But most people take little interest in religious revivals and civic commitments. They lead their lives as best they can, struggling to do things they can believe in and taking responsibility, when they have to, for those near and dear. Communally imposed values tend not to attract the allegiance of people, and there are enough contrary currents in society for people to seek their perfection in divergent ways. The failure of communes provides ample evidence that unity of aim is impossible to achieve even on a small scale. The ideal of society-wide agreement is utopian, and even if we could approximate it, the costs of our comfort would remain untouched.

Something similar is true of the effort to improve our lot by means of prescriptions based on false-consciousness theories. Fortunately, we have actual evidence on hand in this connection. Soviet and other experiments in trying to change the nature, values, and perceptions of people brought great upheavals, but they did not succeed in creating new and more wholesome attitudes to life. If anything, the effects of mediation became more widespread and more noxious. Irresponsibility grew exponentially, manipulation through bribery flourished, and the psychic distance from one's own acts and from one's community became nearly intolerable. The reason is obvious. As power became ever more concentrated in the hands of central authority, mediated chains became ever more momentous, and people felt less and less able to view the actions of political elites as their own. Such overinflated mediated structures collapse under their own weight.

22 Preexisting Values

CONSERVATISM ON THE political right and false-consciousness analysis on the political left approach dealienation with preexisting value commitments. Each offers a vision of what would make for a good life. Each champions a notion of human nature, and each insists on its own hierarchy of values. These views and values are, for the most part, unexamined: they structure what is proposed as the cure of our problems. There is a tendency to consider the values as given and not open to question. Alienation theories present themselves, in this way, as value laden. They reject a cardinal feature of sound theorizing, namely, approaching the facts without a preexisting commitment to their meaning and validity.

Analysis in terms of mediation and related concepts is superior to them because it operates without the claim that we can know what is wrong before we examine the conditions on the ground. Of course, mediation analysis also deals with values, but not values imported into the conversation by theorists. Instead, they are the actual experiences and considered opinions of the people affected by mediation. That individuals suffer when they feel impotent in dealing with government agencies is not an invention but a blatant fact. That even customers have little influence over the lamentable behavior of large organizations can be observed in the rounds of daily living. That being manipulated is a painful reality, that the irresponsibility of others causes untold frustration, and that the inability to appropriate one's actions as one's own can show up as a personality disorder do not require more proof than living in a populous society provides.

There is an important difference between theorizing to express and promote one's values and theorizing to account for the value experiences of people. The former says more about the theorist than about the facts; the latter examines the facts and, with due caution, attempts to account for them. Analysis in terms of mediation and psychic distance shows how the costs of comfort flow naturally from the lives we lead. It doesn't assume which values are worthy and which should be discarded.

It simply accepts the valuations people place on their experiences, attempts to understand their causes, and eventually proposes some strategies for reducing the unwelcome events of life.

This is what I mean by saying that mediation theory is value neutral. It brings no novel notions of good and evil to the table but starts its analysis from the facts that impotence, frustration, irresponsibility, manipulation, and inability to embrace one's actions as one's own are experienced as undesirable aspects of life. It identifies large-scale mediation as the cause of both our comfort and discomfort and proceeds to suggest ameliorative actions. Returns to the past and visions of a utopian future are of little use in making the everyday life of ordinary people better. The forms of reimmediation I suggest here will not eliminate all the noxious effects of the mediated world. But they will lighten the burdens we bear and reduce the cost of our comfort.

The strategies to reduce the undesirable effects of mediation fall into three general categories. The first, consisting of such activities as are required by openness and transparency, aim at increasing the amount of knowledge available to people.

23 Advertising

Since it is both unwise and impractical to try to eliminate mediation, we must develop strategies to reduce its corrosive effects. Advertising, openness, transparency, and education are methods of increasing grasp of the connection between our comfort and our discomfort, the benefits of mediation, and its widespread costs. With enhanced understanding comes the possibility of remedial action: once we know the source of our dehumanization and distress, we can take preemptive steps. The proposed new rules of responsibility are designed to give added social and moral impetus to counteract the destructive effects of mediation. The appeal for immediacy is predicated on the power of fellow-feeling. Many humans display a natural sympathy with others. By an act of imagination, they identify themselves with those who are powerless and suffer. This tendency is by no means universal—the soulless bureaucrat is not a dying breed—but there are enough decent people to begin to make a difference.

Mediation makes specialization possible and fosters it. Specialists develop their own languages, procedures, and technologies. They establish special places—the garage, the courtroom, the hospital—where only they know the rules and the meaning of what occurs. Nonspecialists are outsiders in these worlds; they understand little and are normally denied admission to where these odd but effective rituals take place. They are permitted in when, as patients, clients, or customers, they themselves play a part in the proceedings. But that is the wrong time to try to learn: the sick, the sued, and persons with cracked engine blocks are too anxious and vulnerable to absorb much.

Today, professionals and their clients tend to be cash-connected strangers. It is not in the narrow interest of specialists to let outsiders know a lot about what they do. Openness may lead to having to go beyond meeting peer standards and ultimately to lawsuits, regulation, and loss of revenue. And even if they have only the highest motives, there is no reason to suppose that they know how ignorant their clients or patients are. Mediation creates blindness on all sides. Just as patients cannot even imagine all that doctors know, so doctors have no true sense of the magnitude of patient ignorance. What for the world around them seems shrouded in mystery is daily commonplace to specialists. Being at a great distance from their clients' minds, they find it difficult to understand that things seemingly so obvious could remain unknown.

Ignorance is the natural condition of everyone in the mediated world. The larger the social organism and the more tightly it binds us to one another, the greater our nescience in both scope and depth. This ignorance is of the ultimate form: it is not lack of knowledge about a subject kept in view, but unconsciousness of whole areas of life. In a world such as this, advertising by professionals should not be viewed as primarily a commercial act designed to increase profit, but as a public service activity whose aim is education.

To compensate for the asymmetry of knowledge between professionals and their clients, we have invented the certification of practitioners and of the programs that train them. The premise of such state sanction is that clients and patients are not in a position to find out and to evaluate the quality of service provided by professionals. We lack expertise in what have become highly specialized fields of endeavor, and professionals, like the rest of us, have turned into anonymous strangers in mass society. Certification presumably assures us that these strangers have met peer-sanctioned standards. And professional watchdog bodies, together with the press (which replaces public consciousness), are supposed to make sure that unscrupulous and incompetent operators are exposed and punished.

The sort of openness that can be achieved in large corporations cannot be replicated in the relation between professional and clients. People working for the same company are tied together by purpose and at least a vague understanding of what the corporation does. They can be shown the contributions of their mediating partners, the decisions made by the managers, and the intricate connections of all operating parts, and it is not long before they feel informed and perhaps even supportive of the enterprise. The same technique cannot be employed in counteracting the effects of mediating distance between specialists and their clients. Ordinary people hospitalized and seriously ill are not in a position to profit from revelations of the secrets of diagnosis. They must be reached when they are healthy, and the easiest way to do that is to make the information relevant and attractive.

Although much advertising involves mediation by words or images, it has a unique ability to interest people in whatever they did not think they were interested in. The vital function of advertising by professionals is not to increase profit or to enhance consumer choice, but to educate the people of the mediated world. Viewed from this perspective, it becomes neither an expression of individual freedom nor a sound economic strategy, but a positive obligation to be discharged in the public interest.

It is appropriate to impose this obligation on professionals because they enjoy rich privileges, granted and guaranteed by the community, such as virtual monopoly in their areas of competence. We can reasonably exact a price for such monopolies, and it is particularly fitting that a part of the compensation should be the requirement that protected professionals lift the veil of secrecy shrouding their operations. This suggests immediately that not any kind of advertising will do. Much is notoriously misleading or uninformative. Some aim to create a mood or an image by using suggestive but cognitively irrelevant materials. Evidently, we cannot measure the quality of an ophthalmologist by the eye-popping cleavage of someone dressed as nurse.

It is not that such hype is undignified; rather, it mocks the need advertising should subserve. The consumer needs to know what professionals do, how well they do it, and for how much. Advertising by professionals needs to focus on providing the public with useful material concerning the scope and variety of services offered. To make the services intelligible, there must be information about the needs and conditions that might require them. In this way, physicians, for example, might well convey a wealth of information about health and disease, the proper function and limits of medicine, and the specific content of the subspecialties. It is also appropriate to indicate the behavior expected of professionals, the qualifications of individual practitioners, and the attitude of the advertiser to client-professional relations. Disseminating such useful, factual information is, of course, only a small part of the educational obligations of professionals; the process must be broadened and personalized the moment a new client or patient walks in the door.

This suggests why the obligation to advertise cannot be adequately met in an institutional way. Educational advertising by national and state professional organizations is perfectly acceptable but cannot serve as a substitute for advertising by individual practitioners. Clients and patients need to be informed about the differential qualifications and attitudes of the individuals they contemplate employing. Moreover, education is an intensely personal affair whose success is significantly a function of the communicative interaction of individuals. Advertising by a professional, as the solicitation of such interaction, is the first phase of an intimate, and in many cases tenderly confidential, relationship.

We cannot expect that advertising, even if educational, and the subsequent open and informative interaction between professional and lay persons will by themselves take care of the problems of the mediated world. Mediation impoverishes direct experience; its wide-ranging harmful effects cannot be undone by the presentation of information, open communication among professionals and their clients, and the imaginative extension of the boundaries of the mind. These are useful strategies but no substitute for direct sensory encounter. The words of advertisements are still just mediating words that occupy a central position between people and the realities for which they stand. They can convey information but only invite immediacy. A broad immediacy with others and the world is our best hope of mitigating the fragmentation from which we suffer.

24 Openness

PSYCHIC DISTANCE AND its attendant irresponsibility arise as a result of compartmentalization. In large institutions, employees are assigned narrow roles and required to operate within them. For maximum efficiency, it is best not to look to the right or to the left, experts believe; in a well-designed mediated chain, what coworkers do is not each others' business. The outcome is disjointed vision of a limited routine and active discouragement of inquiry into connections. The image emerging is that of a machine, with each part doing its job and not interfering with the work of the others. This makes ignorance inevitable. Since what anyone does can be understood only from the standpoint of the ultimate product, no isolated act can make any sense. In not knowing the design of the chain and what other workers contribute, employees literally don't know what they do.[1]

Openness is more than the ready sharing of information. It may sound trivial or absurd that in the mediated world, people do not even know all the things they don't know. The appearance of nonsense disintegrates, however, upon a moment's reflection. Of course, people know only what they know and no more. But scientists, for example, are keenly aware of what they don't know, and devote systematic efforts to learning its nature. This is absent in mediation, where coworkers in the same chain know little or nothing of each others' existence and have scant reason to inquire into what they do. This is ignorance in its most vicious form: it limits the scope of knowledge and treats everything beyond it as nonexistent.

The gain through exclusive focus on small tasks is offset by the loss of intelligent commitment to shared goals. The loss is displayed in visible indifference and expressed in such phrases as "What's it to me if the company is doing poorly?" The inability to see the good of the company as coinciding with the good of those who work for it eventually takes a toll on the institution and exposes the search for mechanically conceived efficiency as shortsighted and damaging. Effective participation in the life of the institution begins with enhanced awareness of its values and knowledge of its structure. Whoever thinks that such matters should be reserved for upper management has not experienced the frustration of seeing a business fail.

An early step in overcoming some of the costs of comfort is to expose different links in chains of mediation to one another. If workers learn of the contributions others make, they find it easier to think of themselves and others as engaged in a shared enterprise. Should things not go well, they will be inclined to think that the proper response is to redouble their efforts to find new ways to help. If employees have a clear idea of why what they do is important and what good their labor attains, they are likely to see their interest converging with the interest of their institution. They will be able to appropriate the social act in which they participate as their own and esteem their colleagues as essential and worthy partners.

Mere readiness to disclose the structure of a mediated chain and one's role in it is, therefore, not nearly enough. Years of faceless and unrewarding service make workers indifferent to their employers and interested only in the narrowest interpretation of their jobs. Consequently, we must combat the ill effects of mediation by enlisting the millions serving in government and corporations in wanting to learn more about their situation. Openness is of value only when matched by the will to inquire; without that, goodwill and information go to waste.

A suitable stimulus to inquiry might be exposing every link in a mediated chain to every other. To be maximally effective, this must occur on company time, conveying or reinforcing the idea that coordinated action is in the vital interest of the institution. Once the general idea of interconnectedness takes hold in the minds of people, the free flow of information is likely to provide the details. It is neither necessary nor probable that a fully developed notion of mediation emerge from this immersion. The likely result will be increased grasp of what the company does and, more important, at what human cost.

Sustained exposure to other links in one's chain reveals the irresponsibility endemic to the mediated world and counteracts, at least to some extent, the psychic distance from our acts. It makes it difficult to think of one's narrow role as a harmless way of earning a living. Instead, such exposure suggests an interactive view and encourages feelings of camaraderie. Ultimately, we have to appeal to the unthinking decency of people: when they see the innocence with which we contribute to horrendous acts, they are shocked, recognize their own similar behavior, and tend to institute changes. But significant openness is possible only with the blessing, and in some cases at the initiative of, upper management. Unfortunately, management tends to believe that openness is likely to interfere with its prerogatives and is, in any case, a contributor to inefficiency.

The process of acquainting members of mediated chains with each other must occur not only on a horizontal but also on a vertical level. The chief executive officers of corporations must be familiar with the jobs and with the people who fill the jobs of cleaning the bathrooms. So long as immediate acquaintance is lacking, suspicion falls on fertile soil. The temptation is to develop hierarchical assessments of contribution, celebrating the importance of CEOs and undervaluing the humble work of sanitation. In reality, both sets of tasks must be shouldered, and if we want spotless bathrooms, it may be wise to honor those who scrub them clean.

A similar point can be made concerning politicians. Mayors with grand plans for their communities need to be reminded that quality of life involves a great deal more than attracting professional football to the city. They should ride with the police on patrol to understand the problem of reducing crime and visit every neighborhood to examine the condition of its roadbeds. The reason is not just to bring needed but perhaps small improvements to those who live there, but also to underscore the importance of direct contact with constituents. There are some things that can be learned only by immediate exposure to persons and facts, and with people the instruction is always mutual. The expectation that there is something to be learned from everyone is the foundation of respect for human beings.

The struggle for openness has to involve the attempt to convince management and upper-level civil servants that humanizing mediated chains is of the first order of importance. Openness creates a sense of pride and ownership, enhancing employee commitment. It makes for more informed and generally better customer relations. Further, it increases efficiency by eliminating the reasons for the sullen "I only work here" excuse.

Acquainting employees with the chain of mediation of which the company consists is most effective when it begins directly upon hiring.

An early start acquaints recruits with what they will be asked to adopt as the focus of their waking hours. It introduces them to the jobs of their coworkers, making it impossible for them to remain in the dark about their own contribution. An important element of mitigating the problems of mediation is denying people the opportunity to disappear in organizations as faceless functionaries. We must find a way to have our names inscribed on what we do. That is the only way to combat the anonymity that hides immoral acts.

The ideal to achieve by openness is an intelligent understanding of mediated chains and what they produce. Obviously, not everyone's idea of the purposes and processes of the chains can prevail: institutions cannot act in accordance with everything their members urge on them. This is no secret to sensible people; they do not demand that the world fall in line with their favorite notions. They are satisfied if they get a hearing and an explanation of why their ideas are not as good as alternatives. Not to be taken seriously is one of the great frustrations of human life. A related hurt is not to be considered worthy of being offered reasons for why the organizations to which we belong operate the way they do.

Note

1. My colleague Patrick Shade calls my attention to the following passage from Albert Speer's memoir of Nazi Germany: "The ordinary party member was being taught that grand policy was much too complex for him to judge it. Consequently, one felt one was being represented, never called upon to take personal responsibility. The whole structure of the system was aimed at preventing conflicts of conscience from even arising. . . . Worse still was the restriction of responsibility to one's own field. That was explicitly demanded. Everyone kept to his own group—of architects, physicians, jurists, technicians, soldiers, or farmers." *Inside the Third Reich*, New York, Touchstone, 1970, 33.

25 Transparency

THE MEDIATED WORLD has both more and fewer secrets than we need. There are legitimate uses of secrecy, such as in military preparedness and the private concerns of individuals. In some contexts, the desire to shield information is given full play, and even trivial transfers of knowledge are proscribed. On the other side, government agencies intrude into private lives, and even grocery stores track the purchases and videotape the behavior of their customers. All the parties snooping on each other know that their secrets are most effective if they remain undetected—if, that is, they create the false impression of being transparent.

As a result, much is made of transparency nowadays, especially in politics. Many who use the term acknowledge no distinction between it and openness. But the two terms do not capture the same idea: openness refers to the readiness to share facts, transparency to disclose intentions. In many instances, knowing the underlying purposes is more important than acquaintance with the facts. The reason is that facts often come in miscellaneous bundles; they need to be sorted and made relevant. Purposes provide the unifying ideas that endow facts with meaning, enabling us to understand what is proposed and what is at stake.

Much as physical science insists that the ultimate ingredients of matter display no purposes, the movements of the human world cannot be understood without this central idea. In dealing with our fellows, we need to know what, as we say, they are up to. Without having a clear idea of what others intend, we are unable to understand their behavior. We need to know not only what people do, but also why they do it. This takes us into the realm of values, which is not nearly as mysterious as it may appear. The coin of that realm is labor to attain some ends, investing our activities in something we want. Without an idea of the enterprise on which we are embarked, there is no knowledgeable participation and no standard by which to judge success.

Mediation separates planners from doers and, unless counteracted, restricts intelligent partnership to the ranks of upper management. This is why we need to add transparency to openness if we want to reduce the harmful effects of mediation. Factual information about what coworkers do can leave us in the dark about the history and destiny of the product to whose manufacture we contribute. Pacifists may hold down jobs unaware that they are making parts for hand grenades, and salespeople in the organization may innocently solicit orders for clothes created by child labor.

Lack of transparency adds to the operational leeway of members of the management team. Not having to give an account of what they do and why enables them to achieve purposes that would otherwise be objectionable or at least questionable. When disclosure is unavoidable, the genius of language enables leaders to provide obscure or ambiguous statements about what they intend. Vagueness has become an art in politics, and sometimes the sheer volume of their assertions makes it impossible to get a clear picture of what people mean. Requiring transparency is a mighty step in the direction of learning the intentions that motivate and the actions that satisfy our neighbors.

26 Education

WHEN WE WANT to accomplish something unlikely and difficult, we say that it is a task for education. When it turns out that the desired change cannot be brought about, we say that it is a failure of education. We tend to place unreasonable demands on education, sometimes, no doubt, because we do not have a very clear idea of what it is. That it can do marvelous things is evident from the way it domesticates young savages, endowing them with the resources of some rich tradition. But there are limits to its power: sometimes its gentle persuasion is not enough to wrench people away from their selfish ways.

One may be tempted to think that the steep costs of mediation can be counteracted by some single, simple step. This idea is supported by the human tendency to want to settle issues once and for all. We seem to believe that if a problem is identified with clarity, we can be certain to find its solution. At the time I wrote *Intermediate Man*, for example, I supposed that education would eliminate the problems of mediation. Of course, I did not think that education the way we practice it would do the job; I suggested a number of ways in which what goes on in classrooms would have to be changed. I now think education that stressed sensory experience and immediacy would usefully counterweigh some of the undesirable effects of mediation, but it could by itself not be relied on to turn the tide.

Instead, we need a collection of adjustments whose cumulative influence can bring about the desired outcomes. Education that features direct encounters with the physical and the social worlds promises results, as do changes in the cultures of government and institutions. The growth of openness and transparency, along with the imaginative identification of oneself with suffering others, can accomplish a good deal. Refusal to have one's actions defined by inflexible rules liberates employees to treat humans humanely. There are no magic bullets, but greater awareness of the cost of comfort can reduce the price we pay.

Education is in a particularly strong position to overcome some of the harmful effects of mediation because it exerts its influence over human life at an early stage of its development. Much of what we learn and know derives its authority from the educational system; without major countervailing influences, what teachers say and make one do becomes the norm. Unfortunately, the silent agenda of education is to raise compliant citizens who become team players and accept the cost of their comfort. Lacking an understanding of the power of the system, a few young souls rebel, only to find themselves singled out as troublemakers, sidetracked and on their way to the penitentiary.

A fundamental problem of education as practiced today is the separation of its places, techniques, and rewards from the regular course of life. The schoolroom wrenches students out of their regular milieu, enforces artificial order, and imposes rules of silence. The distance this introduces between education and ordinary life is seen best on the college level in some of the liberal arts, where the sole activity is talking, and the fundamental rule is to be clever. To be sure, some of the readings engage the imagination and expand the mind, but they do so through the mediation of language and at the price of unreality. The imagination is a powerful instrument, but its range is limited by the experience of the person who wields it. The intensity of panic and grief is past our ability to summon up unless we have actually lived through it. People who deny this do so because, not having had the experience, they cannot compare it to what the imagination concocts.

Things stand better with education in engineering, where students come in direct contact with the problems and materials that will occupy them for the rest of their lives. Education in medicine propels students to the bedside, obliterating the distinction between theory and practice. Even such theoretically inclined sciences as physics feature work in labs and thereby endow their abstract theorems with relevance and reality. There were some attempts on the part of humanities disciplines to convert ideas into social reforms, but they were for the most part grand failures. Marxism-Leninism comes immediately to mind as a spectacular disaster, using force and ideology in the quest to change human nature. The modest changes championed by John Dewey would have accomplished more had an entrenched bureaucracy not stood in the way.

The ideal of education is to be universal, requiring that everyone be involved in it and that it occur in an uninterrupted stream throughout the community. If, as pragmatists hold, life is a series of experiments, it is easy to see our transactions with the world as educational. The central ideas to reject are the separation of learning from daily life and the exclusive expertise of educational specialists. The central ideas to embrace are those of lifelong education and the mutuality of learning. Difficult as it is for instructors, the old, and those in leadership positions to accept it, every time they attempt to teach something, their stock of knowledge inevitably also increases.

Once the symmetry of teaching and learning becomes clear, the asymmetry of mediation that separates planners from doers and sufferers is undermined. This does not mean that heads of corporations have to work daily on the assembly line, but it does invite them to profit from regular visits and consultations with ordinary workers. Older people tend to believe that they have seen it all; lifelong education makes it clear that, even though they live in it, they have not seen the new world of the young. The prerogatives of teachers evaporate when they realize how much they have to learn, and leaders acquire humility when they have to turn to their followers for a mandate.

27   The Power of Immediacy

CONSCIOUSNESS IS CUSHIONED in the mediated world. We have eliminated many of the raw experiences of life and have come to believe that pain and disappointment are not necessary events. We have developed pills for physical diseases and medications for what ails the soul. We have moved death out of sight to hospices and hospitals, and unpleasant emotions to the psychiatrist's couch. We acknowledge only what is positive and think we will be able to solve every problem.

This positivity is admirable even if unrealistic. We cannot shield ourselves from every danger and cannot overcome every obstacle. From time to time, we encounter the rough edges of life, but an army of experts is on hand to reestablish our comfort. In this way, we manage to keep the hurtful immediacies of existence at a safe distance. We pay a high price for this ignorant safety: we live as if we inhabited another planet. We lack direct encounter with the forces of the world until the moment they wipe us out. We think in terms of vague generalities and shed our feelings as quickly as we can. We make ourselves believe that we rule the world, if not as individuals, then at least as an excellent species.

Openness, though of great value, does not eliminate mediation. It reduces frustration by creating conditions necessary for communication and understanding. It accomplishes this by the introduction of immediacy, so coworkers and those affected by mediated chains may make accurate assessments of how institutions operate. The hope is that humans seeing humans within the confines of an inhumane system will moderate their behavior in the direction of kindness. Such hope is grounded in the power of immediacy, which shows itself in spontaneous sympathy. A baby in distress tends to move even tough-minded and cruel people. Recognition of the plight of another often results in generous remedial action, and even a simple direct request can bring striking results.

The power of immediacy is best displayed by contrast with ideological generalities. We tend to operate with stereotypes reinforced by prejudice and social exclusion. Each nation has a stereotyped enemy, each religion another faith to fear and crush, and every race at least one other to denigrate. Such hatreds structured a goodly portion of the history of humankind, leading to persecutions, wars, and large-scale exterminations. It is easy to despise others so long as we know them only by collective nouns and in caricature. Muslims and Jews, wops and krauts, blacks and honkies then become objects of disparagement and the butt of jokes. This is the attitude that enables people to say the nineteenth century outrage about Native Americans that "The only good Indian is a dead Indian."

This judgment may seem justified so long as Indians are conceived as standing in the way of western expansion and known only at the barrel of guns. But the legitimacy of even thinking such things disappears the moment we get to know an Indian firsthand as a human being. A blatant contradiction arises: in general, Indians should be killed, but my trusted Indian friend must be helped to flourish. The contradiction resolves itself by the elimination of the stereotype. A moment of recognition wipes the slate clean, and we realize that much of what is said about Indians in general is a lie. They are human beings like the rest of us, with dreams and disappointments and loves and pains.

This is the victory of direct experience over abstract thought. Encountering others without the mediation of ideology makes it possible for people to attend to shared peculiarities and appreciate one another as unique yet strikingly similar individuals. Despite what Hegel argued, sensory experience delivers the particular, and only such living individuals can serve as the foundation of concern and solidarity. Race relations, religious aggression, nationalist ardor, and prejudice against gays are replete with such stories. Stereotypes tend to be smashed by sustained exposure to the humans who, from a distance, looked despicable. Black and white children growing up together are unlikely to fall prey to prejudice, enemy soldiers thrown together in foxholes understand that they face the same sad predicament, and devotees of different religions realize that they worship the same Deity.

The strategy of person-to-person exposure brings results also in the corporate world and in government. Psychic distance from our actions separates us from our mediating partners and even more from functionaries in other chains. We cannot expect universal enlightenment and decency, but the power of seeing distress is striking. The mechanisms underlying it are the identification of self with other and the tendency of misery to spread. The only way to safeguard against sharing the agony of mistreated people is to build walls of indifference, and some bureaucrats manage to do that. But ordinary people allow their emotions to lead them and realize that we all suffer from the same ailments. We struggle with being manipulated, feeling impotent, and living at a psychic distance from who we are. Fortunately, the recognition of our shared predicaments enables us to take steps to reject them. We *can* humanize our interactions.

Mixing races, religions, and nationalities and achieving a level of openness and transparency promote understanding but do not guaranty it. The ultimate chemistry takes place between individuals and cannot be forced. It can, however, be made more probable by providing ample opportunities for experienced togetherness, encouraging antagonists to see each other as seeking the same good and facing similar problems. A great obstacle to overcoming the harm caused by mediation is the growing paucity of direct sensory experience. The rapid development of virtual worlds, communication that does not require bodily presence, and sustained but hopeless attempts to give global scope to sympathy, stretching it beyond its natural limits, all militate against concrete togetherness. The demands of openness and transparency cannot be fully met by word-mediated explanations. We need people in the mediated world to open their minds to understand and their hearts to reject the costs of our comfort.

28 Immediacy and Politics

In societies such as ours, where bureaucratic regulation plays a rapidly increasing role, special attention must be paid to immediacy in public and political life. Decades ago, the president of the United States used to set aside a few hours every week to greet and shake hands with whoever cared to visit the White House. Although these must have been stiff and burdensome occasions, the tradition addressed a need that was urgent and pressing even at a time when we had far less mediation. People who feel impotent and lost in the crowd find it of immense significance to have access to, even in the minimal sense of simply meeting, persons of power. Political scientists may think such desires naive, but psychologists know they are important. Failure to satisfy them has a devastating effect on the body politic: it makes the appropriation of public policies difficult and commitment to them tenuous. Personal contact is symbolic empowerment, and many seek no more. We do not wish to make the tough decisions required of leaders. We want only the opportunity for direct communication, a serious hearing, and frank disclosure of the reasons for the final choice.

A closer look at this communicative immediacy reveals that its essence is educational in the best sense of the word. The hearing afforded ordinary citizens is an opportunity for politicians and bureaucrats to learn from them. And an honest account of the considerations, pressures, and problems involved in the formulation of policy is a better lesson in civics than any school can teach. Viewed in this light, the central task of government is itself educational: it must organize and orchestrate the reciprocal teaching and learning of the community. The ideal is to have as little power-backed regulation as possible. As an absolute minimum, government should forego coercive measures whenever vigorous persuasion or suitable incentives can accomplish the same effect. The vast spread of regulations betokens a loss of faith in the educability of the populace and an absurd confidence that leaders need not or cannot learn anything from dialogues with their constituents.

It is extremely difficult to achieve direct political immediacy in a country as populous as ours. We can attain some results through the personal encounter of politicians with their constituents and of bureaucrats with members of the public they are supposed to serve. Beyond that, we must rely on technological aids that provide a sort of secondary immediacy. Each of us can, at some point, spend some time with elected officials and with civil servants. The demand for immediacy is not so stringent that everyone must meet every representative and each new president: an experience or two, occasionally renewed, provides enough general insight. The informed imagination can then take over and, by generalizing, render the problems of other officeholders vivid and their decisions easier to accept.

In order for the imagination to be informed, however, there must be a steady stream of accurate advice concerning public figures, issues, debates, and policies. The media, especially television with its mediated immediacy, are well adapted to providing this. Seriousness of purpose is the first demand. If both media and politicians believe that their function is to educate adult human beings, sensational revelations, bombastic half-truths, and partisan lies will find less favor in their eyes. The other direction in the flow of information is no less important. Through open complaint sessions, call-ins, public hearings, small group meetings, and questionnaires, but not through impersonal opinion polls, public officials must continually seek instruction from their employers. Such ongoing exchange makes each citizen a full member of the community and enables all to appropriate public decisions as their own.

29 New Rules of Responsibility

WE HAVE ELABORATE rules for holding individuals responsible both for what they did and for what they did not do. We bring people to court for the harm they inflicted on others and even for the threat of harm. There are punishments for acts committed alone and as parts of a criminal conspiracy. We fine people, incarcerate them, and, when the crime is serious enough, we may execute them. Civilized life is built on the security we create by means of a fairly administered criminal justice system. Without such a foundation, brute power replaces right, and no one can go to bed at night assured of being alive in the morning.

Arguably, the greatest threat to morality and to a well-organized, satisfying life is the inability to envisage and deal with the long-term consequences of our actions. Immediate delights outweigh sensible concern about what the future holds, and, if the trouble is distant, people readily throw caution to the wind. Young smokers pay scant attention to lung cancer, and people tend to save for their retirement largely because employers and the government require it. To many, the future seems infinitely far or at least far enough that it does not need to be taken into account. This tendency leads to tragic results: what we had hoped would never happen is soon upon us, and we face a day of reckoning.

Time hides the consequences of our actions and enables us to live in a fool's paradise. Mediation does something similar, except that there our vision is obstructed by other agents and the act-fragment contributions they make to what we jointly bring about. Mediational distance is measured by the number of people necessary to create a social act of some complexity. In making our minuscule contribution to the act, we do not see how it combines with what others do to make a larger whole, and we remain in the dark about the consequences. The resulting sense that we bear no responsibility for what happens destroys the pillars of the moral life and enables people to do what they want heedless of the consequences.

The conditions under which we hold individuals responsible are, for the most part, sensible and sanctioned by many years of experience.

The system fails, however, in relation to mediated actions. We know how to hold persons to account for actions whose intention, execution, and benefits reside in them, but not when they perform only act-fragments. The very nature of mediation sets it against assuming responsibility as we understand it today, enabling agents to claim innocence secured by ignorance.

This irresponsibility gains support from the fragmented nature of mediated actions. Madoff's employees maintained that they were not parties to a colossal fraud; they merely offered bookkeeping services. Guards in extermination camps have sincerely declared that they did not participate in genocide; they simply provided security. Small contributions to a larger, complex act are not identical with the social horror caused. As a result, people who make these contributions can claim blamelessness by pointing to a narrow account of their activities. Sometimes, the claim is self-serving and blatantly fraudulent, but at others, agents are so blindly absorbed in their mediated chain that they appear more as victims than as perpetrators. This appearance has an element of legitimacy: people in mediated chains really do not know what their labor creates. Nevertheless, we cannot allow this to be the last word on the subject. Considering the damage mediation inflicts on social life, even if individuals serving in institutions and government do not know to what they contribute, we can justifiably tell them that they ought to know.

To mitigate some of the costs of mediation, it is precisely this claim to blamelessness that has to be nullified. In order to do so, the rules of responsibility must be changed. Normally, ignorance of the law is not considered an adequate excuse. But other sorts of ignorance sometimes are: we deplore what happens but do not blame parents who leave their child with a longtime neighbor who is an unregistered sexual predator. Part of why we are ready to forgive is that they had no reason to suspect and no way to know of their neighbor's sordid desires.

The "no reason to suspect" and the "no way to know" conditions of sidestepping blame are rarely met in complex social actions. All Madoff's bookkeepers had to do was open their eyes to see the fraud. Extermination camp guards had ample reason to suspect, in the quiet of the night even to know, that they were parties to something horrendous. There are relationships between the two conditions, but they can operate independently. Sometimes, we suspect but cannot know; at others, we know and therefore don't have to suspect. But suspicion demands further examination, and knowledge requires action. At a minimum, decency makes inquiry mandatory: if we want to lead a moral life, we cannot rest satisfied with comfortable ignorance.

To reduce the costs of mediation, we must devise rules for holding every person in a mediated chain responsible for the mayhem caused. Managers in business and government are quick to award kudos to themselves when things go well; the flip side of this must receive equal respect. When some large-scale action results in awful consequences, responsibility for it must be shouldered by everyone who contributed to making it happen. The only excuse to be accepted is unavoidable ignorance, where *unavoidable* means inability to learn what larger act one is supporting in spite of conscientious effort to find out. The assumption behind the stricter rules of responsibility is that unless people know what they spend their time doing and what fruit their efforts bear, they have no incentive to improve their performance.

The new rules of responsibility must be designed in such a way as to make the excuse "I followed orders" unacceptable. When people are hired, the often unspoken expectation is that the new employees will do what their job description demands. Bosses do not welcome many questions. Explorations within one's scope of agency may be tolerated, but inquiries beyond that are read as signs of a meddler. This is the culture that must be recrafted. If employers and employees agreed that apparently innocent activities that lead in their consequences to social damage might land all of them in court, they would start taking a vital interest in the broader repercussions of their actions. They would be inclined to ask for and take advantage of their organization's openness, transparency, and educational efforts.

Of course, there has to be a proportionality to the punishments visited on workers in mediated chains. The decision makers must bear primary responsibility for how the institution operates and for its human failures. But even people in the lowliest position must share the burden, or else there is no hope of moral improvement in the mediated world. Moreover, the punishment must be relatively speedy, to avoid the usual tendency of discounting long-term consequences. Its aim is to acquaint people in mediating institutions with the costs of their behavior and convince them that the usual excuses, such as "It didn't fall to me to make the decisions" and "I didn't know what consequences I was causing," simply will not work.

Concerning momentous events, the world has already moved in the direction of enhanced rules of responsibility. The Nuremberg trials were conducted on the basis of such strict liability, as were proceedings against some Second World War Japanese generals. But individuals lower in the hierarchy were by and large allowed to go free. The idea of applying tougher rules in civil institutions has not found favor in our society. Occasionally, some corporate chieftain is sent to jail for fraud or malfeasance, but ordinary employees of the corporation survive the crisis unscathed. The telephone lines of companies announce that calls are recorded for "quality assurance purposes," but to all appearances nothing much happens to employees who answer the phone in a cheeky or insensitive fashion.

The key to creating a mediated society of growing decency is to deny people the luxury of remaining nameless in their official capacity. Anonymity offers a free pass to office holders to exert institutional inhumanity or to act as they see fit. The moment decency is expected and one has to sign one's name to one's actions, all the requirements of morality acquire life. In holding people responsible for their contributions to mediated chains, we must of course obey the rule of proportionality: we cannot punish single individuals for the shortcomings of the entire chain. But we must make thoughtless actions unpleasant enough not to forget.

Consider for a moment the improvement of the human lot if we required prospective employees to acquaint themselves with the procedures and purposes of the company interested in hiring them. And consider the possibility of a world in which representatives of companies and of the government viewed it as their duty to be competent, friendly, and humane. If education fails to accomplish these changes, rapidly confronting mediating agents with the consequences of their actions may.

Conclusion

THE COSTS OF our comfort grow by the day. Can we turn the tide?

Of course we can. But reducing the cost will take concentrated and difficult efforts of a variety of sorts. Establishing openness and transparency is likely to run into severe resistance. Rewriting the rules of responsibility for a populous society will present special problems. Education will have to be converted into a daily and lifelong affair. The idea that will have to unify this work is that remediation is reimmediation. In large-scale societies, we lose direct contact with the world. That immediacy is what we must regain.

JOHN LACHS is Centennial Professor of Philosophy at Vanderbilt University. He is author of many books, including *Meddling: On the Virtue of Leaving Others Alone* and *Stoic Pragmatism*.